DARE TO LEAD

DARE
TO
LEAD

SECOND EDITION

Pete Pawelek

ISBN-10: 1508805083

ISBN-13: 978-1508805083

Cover design by **David Wickersham**.
        David may be contacted through the author's website, **www.pastorpete.org.**

Book design by **Arc Manor**
        Visit their website at **www.arcmanor.com**

All scripture quotations in this publication are cited from the New English Translation (NET) unless otherwise indicated.

Additional copies of this work and other books by Pete Pawelek may be purchased at **www.pastorpete.org**

Dedication

This book is dedicated to all of the leaders, past and present, at Cowboy Fellowship who have helped me learn these lessons. I am constantly amazed by your dedication and incredible desire to serve and please our Lord. I always remember you in my prayers and applaud your boldness and courage in daring to do the most dangerous task of all, leading!

Special Thanks

I want to offer special thanks to my wife, Abby, and our children Peter, Hadley, and Tatum for their constant inspiration and encouragement. Learning to lead in our home has been the most challenging and pleasurable leadership role I have ever been afforded. Thank you for sacrificing so much not only for this work, but also for the work of the gospel that we are engaged in together. You are the best family I could have ever asked for. I will forever be grateful for your impact on my life and help with this book.

Contents

Why a Second Edition?

This short leadership manual has gone through a number of revisions since it was first written in 2008. None of those changes were substantial enough to constitute a new edition. However, over the past few years, several things have led me to consider updating the guide.

First, I have been through a large number of issues which have helped shape and define what I believe about spiritual leadership. Along the way, I have made mistakes, which have led to a deeper appreciation and understanding of what it means to lead in God's economy.

Since 2008, I have been privileged to witness the growth and development of many other leaders. Some of them were young at the writing of the first edition and are now seasoned leadership veterans. Others have joined our staff, leadership team, or led in various other ways at Cowboy Fellowship. By observing their leadership development I have come to a better (yet still incomplete) understanding of church leadership.

Next, our congregation has tweaked and refined its leadership model during this time period. While our core values, mission, and goals remain, much of our terminology has changed. Words and phrases that were once commonplace at Cowboy Fellowship are now extinct. They have been replaced and refined to better articulate what we believe. Therefore, the terminology from the first manual needed to be updated for clarity and consistency.

There has also been a great demand and numerous requests from other pastors, lay leaders, and churches to have this manual written in a way that can be used in any church. The first edition was written specifically for Cowboy Fellowship, so greater emphasis has been placed on formulating this text for a broader audience.

Finally, the Spirit of God has compelled me to this great undertaking. Writing is difficult and accurately articulating leadership principles is an even more daunting task. Despite sensing a need for this update in 2013, the Spirit of God confirmed it was time in 2015. I have set out to accomplish what I believe to be God's prompting for this second edition.

Introduction

In the fall of 2000, I was selected to lead the outreach team at the Baptist Student Ministry on my college campus. The previous spring I had felt the call from God to serve as a leader. I completed the application and interviewed to be on the leadership team. I had been a leader in my high school, and so I thought to myself, "How much different could leadership in the "church" be?" At our leadership orientation, the BSM director told us we would have ups and downs, success and failure, easy times and hard times along the way in church leadership. Then he said something I have never forgotten, "Remember, leadership is like a minefield. You should be careful where you step or you will get hurt!"

As I considered his statement, I thought, "I did not apply to get hurt. I didn't sign up to walk through a minefield. I just want to serve God!" I thought, "If this is a minefield, why doesn't he tell us where the dangers are?" "Thanks for the warning about the overall danger but what about some specifics?" On my first day as a leader at the BSM, I stepped on my first bomb. Not long after that I hit another, then another, and another. By the end of my first month on the leadership team I felt like I had been hit so many times I was nothing more than a million different pieces laying all over the minefield of leadership. I was ready to quit.

Unfortunately, this is how many leaders feel. When you begin your journey as a leader in God's Kingdom you are excited and ready to do whatever it takes to accomplish what God has called you to do. Then you start going to meetings, filling out paper work, turning in receipts, listening to others complain, not to mention having to deal with the people you lead. Leadership can quickly become frustrating as you try to navigate through the minefield.

That is where this workbook comes in. It will not solve all of your problems nor will it show you where all of the mines are located. No book can do that because the mines of leadership are always moving and constantly changing. Instead, this book will focus on some of the most common things you need to know as a leader. The intent of this book is to give you the tools you need to thrive on the minefield of leadership.

Minefields are dangerous places, but they are more dangerous for some than others. For example, if I was placed in the middle of a minefield, I would most likely sit and pray for help, knowing if I made the slightest move, I would almost certainly die. I have a friend who serves in the military and specializes in minefields. He thrives there because he has the tools and knows how to use them to get himself and everyone else safely through the danger. This book aims to give you some of the most basic tools to get through the minefield ahead.

———— HOW TO USE THIS BOOK ————

This book is best utilized by completing one chapter per week in pairs or in a small group. You might do several chapters in a week and hurry through the study, but you won't have time to really learn how to use the tools that are being offered. So take your time, work slowly, and learn what is in the pages to come.

All leaders need a coach or mentor. After two decades in church leadership, I consult with several other leaders weekly. Through their coaching, they make me a better leader. If you don't have a mentor, seek one out. This may be someone from your church or it could be a great leader from another church. Ask them to walk through this study with you as you begin your leadership journey.

The most important part of this process will be the time you spend with your leadership mentor each week. This person has been where you are going. They will pray for you and help you as you start across the minefield of leadership. Don't be afraid to ask them questions or to call on them as you need their assistance.

Finally, there is a DVD curriculum that corresponds to this study. There are short videos for each chapter to reinforce the main ideas for each leadership topic. The DVDs are available for purchase at www. pastorpete.org.

God has called you to the task ahead and equipped you for the challenges you will face. He has placed others in your path to pick you up, dust you off, and push you forward. You are going to do great, if you dare to lead!

To get the most out of this workbook do the following things:

❖ Read everything
❖ Watch the DVD lessons
❖ Answer all the questions
❖ Review often
❖ Share the things you learn with others
❖ Put the things you learn into practical and use them as soon as possible

CHAPTER 1

——— Leadership is... ———

The saying is trustworthy: If anyone aspires to the office of overseer, he desires a noble task.—1 Timothy 3:1 (ESV)

What is true leadership? This question has been discussed, debated, and talked about for generations. It has been the subject of countless books, articles, and blogs. For centuries men and women have devoted their entire lives and careers to answering the question, "What is leadership?" For those who dare to lead, it is the question that must be answered and understood to have any hope of success in the role of leadership.

If you were forced to define the word leadership with one word, what would that word be? The challenge sounds simple, but if you really sit and think about it for a moment, you will discover that reducing such a powerful term down to a one word definition is more difficult than you think.

Leadership is many things. After years of thinking about what leadership is and after reading countless books, articles, and attending numerous leadership conferences, I believe that leadership should be defined as *influence*. There has never been a leader in the history of the world who was not able to influence people. Leaders must be able to make decisions, act with conviction, endure loneliness, work with others, stay focused, and many other things. However, if they are unable to influence people, their role as a leader will be short lived.

One of my good friends, and one of the greatest men I have ever known, was Clovis Cheatham. Before he passed away in 2007, he told me a story about an encounter he once had with one of the great leaders of World War II. Clovis was unloading supplies one day with some other men on the base when General George Patton walked over and observed the men at work. At the time, they were unloading diesel cans from a cargo truck. Clovis, like all the men, was carrying the cans one by one from the truck to the place they were being stored. Patton walked up to Clovis and said, "Soldier, how many hands do you have?" Clovis replied, "Two, sir!" Patton paused then said, "Then use them both. Two cans at a time from now on!" With that, Patton calmly walked away.

Clovis told me from that day on he never carried just one of anything. For the rest of his life, both hands were always full. That is the power of influence. One might argue that it was Patton's rank, rough attitude, or overall reputation which led men like Clovis to be influenced by his words. But no one can deny it was his ability to influence his men which made Patton the leader he was. One short conversation with Patton influenced Clovis not for a day, month, year, or the duration of the war, but for a lifetime.

This is why the principle of influence is so powerful and important for leaders. Every conversation you have with another person, every action you perform as God's servant, and every act of generosity has the power to influence others. Simply because you are a leader people will listen, watch, and observe everything you do. Your influence will be positive or negative, but you will influence others.

------ **INFLUENCE DISCERNMENT** ------

The power, and importance of influence can be seen throughout God's word from Adam, Abraham, Isaac, Jacob, David, Nehemiah, Esther, Saul, Jesus, Peter, and Paul. They were all leaders in God's Kingdom and all possessed the ability to influence others.

Influence can be achieved in an unlimited number of ways. Most leaders are better at certain ways versus others. Some may find that their ability to speak clearly and eloquently produces the most influence while, for others, it is writing. Still others find their greatest influence through simple acts of kindness and love. Your primary and most natural means of influence will generally be directly related to the way God has hardwired you. Discover and deploy your spiritual gifts, and you will find that they empower you to leverage the greatest influence.

Leaders must also be able to discern with the wisdom God provides which means of influence is best suited for the situation in which they find themselves. A leader who cannot understand the value of this concept with a discerning spirit will regularly find himself being torn apart in the process of leading.

My spiritual gifts are centered in preaching, teaching, and administration. As a result, my influence is primarily through speech, writing, and the ability to delegate and empower others. At church, my leadership is primarily based on my ability to communicate with other leaders in an effective way.

However, to be an effective leader in my home, discernment and common sense must be applied. My three children don't enjoy forty-five minute sermons right after dinner. My wife is not fond of me delegating tasks for her to complete on a daily basis. To be an effective leader in my home, it is necessary that I practice a different kind of leadership.

This is true for other roles I participate in each month. I serve on several boards of directors, for example. As a board member, people want to know what I think, but I have no power to delegate. I am also rarely afforded the privilege of opening the Bible and dissecting a few verses to prove my points. Instead, I am expected to listen, pray, and then quickly articulate any points I feel important enough to raise. Once my opinion has been expressed, the extent of my influence has been exhausted in these situations.

If I expect to have any influence at all in my home or as a board member, I must be able to discern what actions, words, or services give me the best opportunity to be a person of influence. What works with one person or in one situation will most likely not work in all cases.

——— YOUR SPHERE OF INFLUENCE ———

Through two decades of leading and observing other leaders, it has become clear that all leaders have a sphere of influence and most leaders fall into one of two extremes. The first group drastically *under*estimates the size, and the second drastically *over*estimates the size of their sphere. One is more common in young leaders and the other in seasoned leaders.

While some young leaders arrive on the scene with a bravado that implies they are the next apostle Paul, most are timid and nervous. As a result, they underestimate their sphere of influence. They are cautious, deliberate, and move at a painstakingly slow pace. After all, they are on a minefield. Their motto is, "If I move very slowly, I won't get blown up." The problem with this approach is they never get to where they are going.

The difficulties with those who underestimate their sphere of influence are numerous. First, most people view leaders who are cautious, deliberate, and slow movers as being unsure and incapable in their leadership. As you will learn later in this work, the ability to articulate a vision and move toward that vision is vital for all leaders in the process of developing influence. Those who do not dare to lead, and engage those in their entire sphere of influence will quickly notice that the number of people following will begin to dwindle. Naturally, this will reduce their sphere of influence.

The second problem with leaders who underestimate their sphere is that they can fall into the excuse trap. This leader always has a reason why he or she has not been able to accomplish what God purposed in his or her heart to do. The reason they fail many times finds its root in underestimating their sphere of influence. When a leader fails to utilize every member in their sphere, less is accomplished and as a result, the leader feels compelled to present an excuse.

If God has called you into leadership and birthed a divine vision in your heart, then lead with vigor and intensity. Don't discount your commission as a leader, rather embrace it and run your race well. Don't underestimate God's purpose for your role as a leader. Don't underestimate the size of your sphere of influence.

The second kind of leader is the polar opposite from the first. Generally, they are more seasoned leaders. Many times, they have held leadership roles in the secular world, politics, or church. They are confident, ready, hard charging people with all the answers. They think they can shape, change, and control everything. Their motto on the minefield is, "If I run really fast, I can't get hurt." The problem is they always blow themselves up, and they frequently hurt many others in the process.

Typically, people enjoy following this type of person for a period of time. However, once the bombs start going off, those following tend to back off or drop out of the race altogether. Sometimes the pace these leaders set is too difficult for others to follow. They are high-energy people with high expectations for any who are on their team. While these things can be beneficial in the right doses, these leaders generally don't take the time needed to administer the right amounts of influence.

Problems also arise with these types of leaders when they find they can't change, shape, or influence something. When they are faced with the truth that not everything is in their sphere of influence, it becomes an unacceptable reality. When the church does not vote their way, or the pastor won't push their agenda, or the budget does not reflect their values, these leaders frequently push the self-destruct button as they walk out the door.

The truth is that no one has an unlimited sphere of influence. Some have larger spheres than others, but everyone has boundaries when it comes to the way he or she can influence others. Even the President of the United States, who is considered by most to be the most powerful man in the world, has limits. While the sphere produced by that grand office is global, it has been unable to influence countries like North Korea and Cuba for decades. Presidents from both parties have frequently had trouble influencing the Congress and Senate, and State leaders to embrace their ideas and follow their leadership. No sphere of influence is limitless.

Thriving in the minefield of leadership requires a leader who is able to clearly discern and leverage his or her sphere of influence. This leader is able to move fast enough to get somewhere, but slow enough for others to follow and avoid dangers along the way. Finding the right pace is crucial on the minefield of leadership.

Finally, all who dare to lead must realize that neither value nor potential as a leader is determined by the size of your sphere of influence. A leader of tens will have more influence than a leader or thousands in many cases. Recognize and embrace your sphere of influence; do your best not to underestimate or overestimate it. Finally, find true contentment in your God-given leadership responsibilities despite its size or perceived potential.

——— EARNING INFLUENCE ———

The ability to influence those around us must be earned. As a leader in the church and God's Kingdom, you must never assume that influence will automatically be granted because of a title before or after your name. Some will allow you to influence them for a short time because they respect your title or position. They assume because you are a "leader" that you are the type of person they should submit to and be willing to be influenced by. As a result, they will respect you as a leader for a period of time simply because of the title or position you hold. However, you must still earn their trust and the right to continue to influence them.

How do you earn the right to lead and influence people? The answers to this question are as broad and varied as the answers to the question, "What is leadership?" We can, however, give some general guidelines on how to earn the respect of others and the right to lead and influence their lives.

First, you must care about those you lead. Proverbs 27:23 says: *Be sure you know the condition of your flocks, give careful attention to your herds.* Leaders in the Bible are often referred to as shepherds. Shepherds always know the condition of the sheep they lead. My father is a farmer and rancher, and it always amazes me that he knows the condition of his herds and fields at all times. When my parents travel for short vacations, my dad often asks me to feed or check on his herd at the homestead. These forty cows and their calves represent a small portion of his entire herd, yet when I call him to report on their condition, I always do it while I am still with the herd because his questions are so specific. He will ask questions about the front right hoof of a certain cow or about how any one of the calves in the herd is walking or nursing. Every time I think I have caught something new and call to report it, he usually already knows about it. He knows the condition of his herd.

My father cares about his herd and has devoted his life to leading them. When the herd sees my father's truck coming, they rush toward him. When they see my truck coming, they hardly notice. My father has earned the right to influence them. It has been said, "People don't care how much you know until they know how much you care." All who dare to lead must understand this. If you don't care about those you lead, your ability to influence them will be limited.

Next, you must be trustworthy. In his work, "Leadership Is The Key," Herb Miller cites honesty as one of the key character traits people want in their leaders.[1] No one in a volunteer organization like a church is willing to follow someone they cannot trust. Those who lie, cheat, manipulate, or mislead will not last long as leaders in God's church. Those who attempt to hide or keep all the information to themselves rarely excel in leadership roles in part because people feel those leaders cannot be trusted. They are perceived as being dishonest. If people do not trust you, they will not allow you to have influence over their lives. Look at the kinds of leaders Jethro advised Moses to select:

> Exodus 18:21 (NET)—[21]*But you choose from the people capable men, God-fearing, men of truth, those who hate bribes, and put them over the people as rulers of thousands, rulers of hundreds, rulers of fifties, and rulers of tens.*

Leaders must fear God, be trustworthy, and hate dishonest gain! If people do not trust you, they will never follow you. If people cannot believe you when you speak, they will never listen to you. As a leader, you must be trustworthy. You must go above

---

1   Herb Miller, Leadership Is The Key (Nashville, Tenn: Abingdon P, 1997), 55.

and beyond to ensure that you never give anyone any reason not to trust you. Should you lose the trust of an individual or team you are leading, you must stop everything, suspend all other activities, and deal with the issue of trust immediately. You must regain the trust of those you lead or run the very real risk of losing the influence you have worked so hard to gain.

A leader must also communicate with those they lead to earn the right of influence. Communication is hard work. It takes time, patience, persistence, and practice, but all leaders must understand the value of communication. If a leader is a poor communicator, then three things will happen.

The first thing that comes with poor communication is confusion. If you don't communicate with others you lead, they will become confused on the vision, direction, and mission of your ministry or task. Those you lead cannot read your mind, so you must always practice good communication to keep those you lead from becoming confused.

The second thing poor communication does is cause others to stumble. Poor communication incites anger, gossip, and will even drive people to quit on a task that God has given them to complete. Poor communication can also cause people to second guess their leader.

Finally, poor communication decreases confidence. If you don't communicate well, others will not have confidence in your leadership skills and ability. They may think you are hiding things from them, which causes them to lose trust. They might just think you don't know what you are doing. Even if that is true, communicate that you are unsure to your team. Ask for their help, be open about your struggle to discern God's will for the team. They will be more likely to respect you for your clear communication and honesty and continue to follow you.

The final thing I would suggest leaders must do to earn the right to influence others is be available to those they lead. Those you lead need your time. People know you love them when you make time for them. J. Oswald Sanders writes, "The quality of a person's leadership will be in part measured by time; its use and its passage."[2] As a leader,

---

2   J. Oswald Sanders, Spiritual Leadership Principles of Excellence for Every Believer (New York: Moody, 2007), 93.

you must make a point of managing the 24 hours of a day. While your responsibilities and leadership roles grow, the seconds, minutes, and hours in the day will not. The problem leaders face often is not that they don't have enough time, rather it's that they fail to properly use the time they are given. God will not give you more than you are able to bear. He has given you sufficient time to accomplish His tasks. Leaders must not waste time, or they will have none left to give to those they lead.

The greater your leadership role and influence, the more intense this battle will become for you. A leader of ten will have more time for each person he or she leads than a leader of one hundred. A leader of one thousand or ten thousand will have to be extremely selective when it comes to using his or her time properly. Time is valuable and those you lead know it. When they need to talk, vent, or brainstorm, they will want your ear. When things are going bad at work, home, or in some other area of life, they will call upon you and need your time. You must be willing to make yourself available to those you lead. As a leader, you will be called to give up many things. Time is only one of them.

Depending on the size of your group, you may not be able to make yourself personally available to everyone you lead, but every effort should be made to ensure that those you lead have someone to talk with when they need help. You can earn influence by making yourself available, and you can lose it by doing the opposite. Leaders don't have more time, but what sets them apart is the way they manage the time they are given.

LOSING INFLUENCE

Influence is extremely hard and costly to earn; however, it is also very easy to lose. A leader must guard his ability to influence others at all times. Without influence, a leader's ministry will be stifled or even destroyed. Take Moses, for example. He is one of the greatest leaders in the Bible. His life has been the subject of many leadership studies, and his life as a leader can be an example for each of us. His ability to influence others with his God given gifts is amazing. However, we can also see a time in his life where he lost influence.

In the book of Exodus, we find the story of Moses' early life in Egypt. A Hebrew child saved from infanticide and raised in the house of Pharaoh, Moses undoubtedly was well-known around town. While we can't know for certain, one can easily conclude that Moses knew he was different than his mother and those who lived in the palace with him.

For starters, he looked different. He was not Egyptian; he was a Hebrew. Moses must have struggled seeing his fellow Hebrews work as slaves in the heat of the Egyptian sun. Each day, his brothers and sisters were tortured, maimed, and killed doing the work of Pharaoh. All the while, Moses enjoyed the power and influence of being a member of the royal family. One day while out watching the Hebrews work, he observed an Egyptian beating one of the slaves. Attempting to do the right thing, Moses defended the Hebrew and ended up killing the Egyptian. How much influence Moses had with the Hebrews at this time in his life is not clear. However, we can see that whatever influence he might have had was gone the following day. Moses was near the Hebrews work site, and this is what the Bible records:

> **Exodus 2:13–14 (NET)**—[13]*When he went out the next day, there were two Hebrew men fighting. So he said to the one who was in the wrong, "Why are you attacking your fellow Hebrew?"* [14]*The man replied, "Who made you a ruler and a judge over us? Are you planning to kill me like you killed that Egyptian?" Then Moses was afraid, thinking, "Surely what I did has become known."*

Due to the murder the previous day, Moses lost whatever influence he once had with the Hebrews. Furthermore, he lost all influence with Pharaoh and the royal family. His influence was gone, and his only hope of survival was to flee Egypt.

All leaders can learn a lesson from Moses. Be careful how you act, what words you use, and the way you live your life. All of the influence you have worked hard to earn can be gone or reduced dramatically very quickly. This often happens when we are trying to do the right thing. Most leaders have good intentions, but even good intentions can lead to a loss of influence. A loss of influence always leads to a loss of leadership potential.

There is an encouraging lesson to be learned in the story of Moses and his leadership journey. All leaders know, or will learn that God is in control. Moses learned from the incident in Egypt, and God used him to free the Hebrew people and lead them out of Egypt many years later. A loss of influence does not mean you can never lead again. It just means you might spend some time in the desert.

──── **CHAPTER SUMMARY** ────

Leadership is many things, but at its core and in its simplest state, leadership is influence. All great leaders are great influencers. Leading people and influencing people are not easy tasks and can quickly become frustrating. Paul put it this way: *Here is a trustworthy saying: If anyone sets his heart on being an overseer, he desires a noble task.*[3]

Being an overseer or leader is indeed an honorable task. It will not always be easy or fun; however, it is always worth it. God has gifted you and prepared you for the task ahead. He never gives us more than we can bear. You can do this, so long as you understand that your role as a leader is to influence those God places in your care. In the coming chapters, we will discuss many more principles about leadership, but none are more important than understanding the power and purpose of influence.

Final Questions

1. Think again about those people who have influenced you. How did they earn that right?

2. List some people you feel you have influenced in the past. How did you earn the right to lead and influence them?

3. Can you think of some examples of people who misused their influence in leadership roles?

---

3   1 Timothy 3:1 (NIV84)

4. What are some things that can cause you to lose your influence?

5. What should you do if you lose your influence?

6. If you lose your influence in the future, or have lost it in the past, does this mean God can no longer use you? Why or why not?

7. Think about those you are or will be leading. How can you show them you care? How do you tell them you care?

8. What are some things that cause leaders to lose the trust of those they lead?

9. What should be the reaction for leaders when trust has been lost with those they lead? Why?

10. Why is understanding your sphere of influence important? Can you make a list of people who are inside of your sphere of influence? Is your sphere bigger or smaller than you thought?

CHAPTER 2

_____ What Does a Leader Do? _____

I will give you leaders who will be faithful to me. They will lead you with knowledge and insight.—**Jeremiah 3:15** (NET)

I f leadership is influence, the question is, "How do we do it?" What must a leader do in order to influence others? The model Jesus gave is straightforward and simple, however, it is often overlooked. Jesus was the greatest influencer and leader the world has ever known. His influence has lasted throughout the ages, and despite his physical absence from our planet for over 2000 years, his leadership still guides believers today. It must be noted that today Jesus speaks to believers and leads through the Holy Spirit. However, ultimately we are still led by the words He spoke and lessons He taught while he traveled the dirty, dusty, roads of our world. Jesus did five things that leaders must learn in order to succeed in leadership roles.

The first thing leaders do is *model* or *show* others the way. Great leaders set the example for others to follow. They go first and never ask others to do a task or mission they would be unwilling to take on themselves. Jesus set the example for his disciples to follow. He did not practice what he preached; instead, He preached what He practiced. Jesus was not the kind of leader who spoke and expected people to respond. He motivated others by his actions and his willingness to lead the way.

Jesus did not preach on prayer and then go practice it. He practiced prayer and then taught the disciples when they asked about it. He preached about what He had already practiced throughout his ministry. Leaders in God's Kingdom today are no different. They lead the way. They are models that others desire to become, not because they are smart, rich, or well-spoken, but because they look like Jesus. They understand the power of preaching only what they have already practiced.

The second thing leaders do is *inspire others*. The inspiration Jesus provided was not solely through grand speeches or well crafted teachings. His inspiration came from the ability to help others see the future and the vision that God had for their lives. Jesus often spoke about "The Kingdom of God." This future vision inspired people. Today's leaders must inspire those they lead. This begins with helping others see the overall vision and mission God has given the church and how that matches up with God's vision for all of mankind. In the following chapter, the importance of understanding the mission and overall purpose of your church will be discussed. A leader cannot inspire others to their fullest potential until the mission and purpose are understood.

In college, I met a student who did not know the Lord; however, over the course of a few months and developing a friendship with her, she gave her life to Christ. She was baptized, started to attend church, and was on her way in her new life with Christ. One day, about 5 months after her conversion, she said to me "I don't know what I am supposed to do with my life anymore." I took this opportunity to attempt to inspire her. "What do you think God's plan for the world is?" I asked. She responded by talking about the Great Commission and shared how she felt God wanted all of mankind to have an opportunity to understand and respond to the Gospel. We talked about that for some time, elaborating on the overall vision and mission God has given Christians and the church. I said, "Jessica, you have an incredible gift and passion for the lost, and I believe God is going to use your talents in some incredible way to accomplish his vision and mission for our world." She replied, "Really? God can't use me, can he?" Now, all these years later, I am pleased to report that Jessica is serving in a remote foreign land as a missionary and has had part in leading many to Christ. Just before she left for her first term as a missionary, she called and told me how much that conversation had inspired her. All I did was help her see into the future and understand the mission and purpose of the church.

You don't have to have long, drawn out, well prepared sermons or speeches to inspire those you lead. The truth inspires people. Simply speak truth into their lives. Talk about the amazing plan God has for mankind and how God can use the individual you are leading in that plan. That alone is enough to inspire those we lead.

Leaders model and inspire those they lead, but they also *challenge* their followers. Most humans respond well to challenges. We are accustomed to them, and we have grown to expect them in all areas of life. In grade school, we are challenged to learn, fit in, do well in sports, and interact socially. In college, we are challenged with many of the same things as grade school, but new challenges are added. During the young adult years, we are forced to find out who we really are as people without our parents. We are challenged to think "outside of the box" and leave our comfort zones in many areas of life. Upon graduation and entrance into the "real world," we are challenged to find jobs. Once in our new roles, we are challenged to learn the ropes, climb the ladder, and provide for our families. It is in the face of challenges that we seem to excel in life. When we are pushed to the limit, we do our best work and become stronger and healthier people in the process. The two areas in life many are never challenged, are in their faith and congregational responsibility.

Don't you find it strange that people are willing to be challenged in every area of life, but when it comes to church and faith, they simply want to sit back and do nothing? Or do they? Churches in the last few decades have bought into this lie. The fact is people do desire to be challenged at church and in their spiritual lives. When you challenge those you lead to connect, grow and serve in the Kingdom, most will rise to the challenge.

Jesus did this with the disciples on many occasions. Take the feeding of the 5,000 for example. Who fed the people that day? You might be tempted to say Jesus, but in fact, it was the disciples who fed the people. It was the disciples who were challenged to first come up with a solution to the problem. They found a boy with some bread and fish but not enough to feed the hungry and extremely large crowd. After blessing the fish and loaves, Jesus challenged them by telling the disciples to distribute the food. Jesus challenged their faith that day! As a leader, Jesus understood the power in challenging those he led.

He also understood the cost of challenging people. In John 6, many of those following Jesus turned back because they perceived his teachings to be too hard and challenging. If you dare to challenge those you lead, some will turn back. However, it should be noted that the few who rise to the challenge will be more effective than the many who sit and do nothing at all. Don't be afraid to challenge those you lead when it comes to their faith!

It is important to understand that challenging those you lead comes in many shapes and forms. The idea is not to push them to the breaking point. People today have enough on their plates and going on in their lives. The idea behind challenging others is to help them grow in their faith, not give them more to worry about or do. When a leader challenges someone, there must be a purpose behind it. Do you remember my friend Clovis who was challenged and inspired to carry two cans at a time? There was purpose behind that challenge. Good leaders don't challenge those who follow without purpose. You must also try not to challenge everyone in the same way. Some accept challenges better than others. Some are able to take on more than others. As a leader, your job is to figure out how you can best challenge those you lead to help them grow in their faith.

Finally, don't attempt to challenge others if you are not being challenged yourself. Good leaders are always challenging themselves. They surround themselves with people who will challenge them to grow, learn, and excel in all areas of life. Leaders must dare to be challenged before they can attempt to challenge others.

The fourth thing good leaders do is *encourage* those they lead. Challenge without encouragement, even with a model and inspiration, will only lead to frustration and burnout. Often leaders fail to encourage those that surround them. The demands of leadership are tiring, and encouragement takes effort and energy that we don't always have to offer at the end of a day or week. This is no excuse. We must encourage those we lead.

This is a weak point in my personal leadership skill set. I am not naturally a person who thinks to encourage others. While I enjoy encouragement in my own life, I am not one who needs much of it to carry on with the tasks I have been given. Some would say I am "low maintenance." Since I don't require much encouragement in my own life, I often forget that others around me need it in theirs. The lack of sensitivity in this area of leadership has caused me to lose influence and the ability to lead many people over the years. Through much pain and personal reflection I have come to the conclusion that this weak spot in my leadership skill set will limit my ability to lead if I never dare to address it. I will only be as effective in leadership as I am in encouragement because this is my weakest link.

Each leader is naturally strong in certain areas. Perhaps you are great at inspiration or challenging people. Those things will not limit your leadership. The area you are weakest in will limit your leadership. If your weakest area is modeling, you will never be a better leader than your ability to model will allow. Therefore, you must work on that area of leadership to increase your overall effectiveness as a leader in God's Kingdom. It is important to identify your weakest area and work at it with all your heart. Allow God to change that attitude or area of your life. Transform that weak area and your leadership will be transformed as well.

Encouragement can be accomplished with a short note, quick phone call, email, public recognition, and other various ways. Take the time and put forth the effort to encourage those you lead just as Jesus encouraged those he challenged.

The fifth thing good leaders do is *empower* those they lead. Jesus not only modeled, inspired, challenged, and encouraged the disciples, but he also enabled them to do ministry. He was willing to let things go, delegate, send them out, and allow them to fail. Leaders who do the first four things we have discussed but are unwilling to dare to empower those they lead never reproduce themselves and never reach their full leadership potential. The goal of Christian leadership is not just to lead people to Christ and teach them how to work. Jesus wants us to empower those we lead as well.

Jesus sent the disciples out two by two. With 2,000 years of experience behind us we think, "Wow! What a great idea." But at the time, had we been consulting Jesus, I fear that many of us would have said. "WHAT ARE YOU DOING? Peter has a loose tongue, Thomas has little faith, these two over here are always fighting like children, and Judas is shady at best and a crook at worst. Don't send these guys! They are going to embarrass you and ruin your reputation!" Jesus understood something that many leaders do not. Leadership is not leadership until you are willing to let go of something yourself and empower others to carry out the task and mission.

For years, I was convinced that I needed to be at everything. Set up, clean up, every meeting, every funeral, wedding, birth, hospital visit, phone call, office problem, outreach event, ministry event, workday, and the list goes on and on. One day, God revealed that this was not leadership; it was micro-management. When I learned the value of letting go and empowering others, my leadership went to another level, and our church followed. Empowering others allowed our church to minister and reach our community with the Gospel of Christ in a more effective way. You must not try to empower the team or individual too fast by throwing everything at them all at once. This fifth step is a process that may take weeks, months, or years depending on the size of the ministry and maturity of those you are leading. In many cases, empowering others can be fully accomplished in six months to a year. In some larger and more complex ministries, it may take longer, but rarely should it take more than two years. Empowering others is the final step in the Biblical model of leadership.

There will be a period of time that your presence, attention, and leadership will be required in order for the ministry to succeed. However, if after twelve to twenty-four months, your ministry cannot function without you, beware; you are most likely managing your team rather than leading it.

——— **CHAPTER SUMMARY** ———

Leaders model, inspire, challenge, encourage, and empower those they lead. Doing these five things is what separates a leader from being nothing more than a supervisor or manager. God has not called you to manage and supervise; he has called you to lead! Leaders do many things, but at the core of each of the leader's tasks, you will find these five things that good leaders do.

Final Questions

1. How many leaders do you know that do all five of these things?
2. Out of the 5 things leaders do, which one are you weakest in today? Why is that important?
3. How can you empower people to do the ministry?
4. In an effort to empower your team, why should you not just throw it all in their laps at one time?
5. How long do you think it will take you to get your team to the stage where they can do the ministry with or without you?
6. What does it mean to preach what you practice? Give an example.
7. What inspires you? Do you think that will inspire others?
8. List some times or ways Jesus inspired those he led.
9. What are some things you can challenge those you lead to do? Think of real people and real examples.
10. Why is challenging others important?
11. Honestly, would you say you need a lot, some, a little, or next to no encouragement personally?
12. How will this affect the way you encourage others?
13. Have you ever been challenged without encouragement? How did that feel?

CHAPTER 3

——— **Mission & Values** ———————

> *Therefore go and make disciples of all nations, baptizing them in the name of the Father and the Son and the Holy Spirit, teaching them to obey everything I have commanded you. And remember, I am with you always, to the end of the age.*"—**Matthew 28:19–20** (NET)

A leader is one who influences others. This influence takes on many different forms depending on the organization in which the leader finds himself. For example, in the military, leaders influence those under their command to fight and perhaps die for a cause. In a corporate or business model, leaders influence those they lead to make a profit and please the customer or investors. In the family, parents influence their children to become fine upstanding adults and productive members of society. In the church, leaders attempt to influence those we lead to become disciples of Jesus Christ. As a leader in God's church, your goal should be no less. Those under your leadership should be encouraged and influenced in the direction of discipleship.

——— **THE PROBLEM** ———

Leadership in the church is more difficult than leadership in any other area of life. This is why many great business leaders, military leaders, and family leaders make poor leaders in the church. This is also why many of the greatest leaders the church has ever known were never successful leaders in the secular world. Leadership in the Kingdom of God is much different than leadership in the kingdom of man. These two types of leadership share some things in common, so similarities can be found. The leader in the church, however, is faced with a problem that secular leaders rarely encounter. The problem can be summed up in one word: volunteer.

Those we lead in the secular world are paid or compensated in some tangible way. They are easier to lead because they desire to keep their jobs, receive their paychecks, and get promoted. While we receive an eternal reward for our work inside the Kingdom of God, the rewards are often not immediate and the work does not always seem worth the effort and sacrifice it requires. Due to this, volunteers are less reliable, less dedicated, and need more direction and motivation than those we lead in the world outside the church.

It is easy to become frustrated and angry when volunteers fail to show up on time or don't show up at all. The job they were assigned may still get done, but one can see that it was only partially or half-heartedly completed. Then a leader is faced with asking the question of why this happened. Leaders frequently blame the volunteers and criticize them for not caring about the church or the mission they were to complete. These leaders sometimes accuse volunteers of being lazy and many other things that are, in many cases, partially true. However, the leader should always start with self-reflection when they find problems with volunteers.

As a leader, did you cast the vision for the mission? Did the volunteers understand the significance of their task? Was the leader clear and consistent with his or her communication? Volunteerism will only thrive in conjunction with great leadership. Anything less almost always leads to frustration and failure. Those you lead are *volunteers*, which will demand that you take your leadership to another level. To take your leadership to that level, you must first know and understand the mission, values, and structure of your church.

MISSION

The overall mission of most Christian churches is the same. In its simplest and most generic form, we might say it is to fulfill the great commission of Jesus Christ by winning the lost and making disciples. In the first edition of this manual, I included the mission and values of Cowboy Fellowship (the church I pastor) in this section. In this edition, though, I have intentionally made the choice to omit those paragraphs for two reasons.

First, while our overall mission to win the lost and make disciples has not changed at Cowboy Fellowship, the way we understand and are now attempting to fulfill that mission have changed in the last five years. After witnessing the slow transition that has taken place at our own church over the past decade, I was inspired to talk to other pastors about their experiences. Almost all of the churches I spoke with on the topic stated that their understanding and methodology for winning the lost and making disciples had changed in some significant way in their tenure at the church. Therefore, it is an impossible task to explain something that is constantly changing.

Second, all churches differ in some ways when it comes to mission. The context, culture, geographical location, denomination, and numerous other matters greatly affect the way a church understands mission. Therefore, it would be unwise for me to assume I can speak for your church on the subjects of mission or values. Instead, your church most likely already has a handout, leadership supplement, or other means to express its mission. Why not spend some time this week examining the mission of your church with your pastor or leadership coach?

WHY THIS IS IMPORTANT

As a leader in your local congregation, it is imperative that you understand the mission, values and structure of your church. People will ask you questions, present you with challenges, and expect you to speak on some level for your congregation. This will come from those inside and outside of your church. Therefore, it is vital that you understand what your church believes, teaches, and attempts to accomplish as a congregation. Simply gaining a full understanding of your congregation's mission, values, and leadership structure will give you more confidence and authority when you speak as a leader in your community.

According to Ford, there are six basic levels to learning. They are knowledge, comprehension, application, analysis, synthesis, and evaluation.[4] It is important that you learn the mission, values, and leadership structure of your church at the highest level which is evaluation.

As a leader, you should do much more than simply memorize the mission statement of your church. However, this is sadly what most leaders do. They memorize but fail to fully comprehend their congregation's methods and means of ministry and mission. Rather than aiming to memorize, you should seek a higher level of comprehension.

It is important that you dissect and really dive into the mission of your church. Ask questions; seek to understand how the values of your church work in real life. Analyze how your ministry team or committee can help uphold these values. Sit down and talk with your pastor or leadership coach and attempt to really apply the mission of your church to the context of your ministry. This is a very important process that will not be short but must not be overlooked.

If you want to be successful as a leader, you must understand the mission of your church and be able to fully articulate it to those you lead. If you don't understand the mission of your church, you will find it difficult to speak with authority when you are asked to articulate the mission of your team. If you can't explain the mission, you will find it very difficult to gain the support of your followers.

The highest level of comprehension in Ford's model is evaluation. At this level of understanding, you not only know what the mission is, but you can explain it and identify it. Many times leaders are asked a question that goes something like this. "Why does our church..." Leaders many times say something to the effect of "well because we

---

4   LeRoy Ford, *Design for Teaching and Training* (Nashville: Broadman Press, 1978), 101.

love Jesus." Or "Because the Bible says we should…" While those answers may be correct they are not complete, and as a result the questioner leaves unsatisfied.

When operating at the level of evaluation the leader is able to break the mission apart and explain it down to the very last detail. They are also able to identify how the mission is being fulfilled. For example lets say the mission of your church is "to make disciples." It's one thing to be able to explain how the discipleship program is accomplishing the mission, but can you explain the how the greeting team, nursery workers, arena ministry, or garden club are all working together to make disciples? Leaders in the church should attempt to understand the mission of the church in its larger context, not simply in regards to whatever ministry team they lead.

If all leaders in the church would take the time to learn the mission of their church at this depth, and consider how the entire Body is accomplishing the mission, the church becomes much stronger. Learn about the mission of your church, evaluate it, ask questions about it, and then share it with everyone else.

——— VALUES ———

It is equally important that team leaders understand the values of their churches. While the overall mission of the church provides direction, our values help us decide how to handle situations and issues that surface along the way as we attempt to accomplish the mission. A church's values should be written down, and all leadership should understand and be able to apply them to their own ministries.

Here is why knowing your church or organization's values is important. Most companies and large organizations in the secular world have two things in common when it comes to their values: safety and customer service. If an employee is dealing with a customer service issue and this employee sees another customer getting ready to slip and fall on a wet spot on the floor, then the employee has a decision to make based on the values of the company. If safety is the number one value, then he will stop tending to one customer in order to keep another customer safe. If there is no order to the value system, then the employee may continue to serve the customer while another customer breaks an arm or leg.

What we value helps us to determine the order in which we do things and how we handle situations. If we value church, we make it a priority in our lives, so church overrides other things. If we value fun and recreation over church, we will spend most Sundays doing those things, only getting to church when we have time. It all comes down to values. A leader must understand the values of the church to effectively lead.

When we speak of values in the context of church, we are speaking of spiritual values. Of course, every church values safety and other commonsense physical things that affect its members. Specifically for the purpose of training leaders, though, we want to look at the spiritual values of a church.

As was the case with mission, you should find that your church has a unique set of values. Talk with your leadership coach or pastor about these values. If they are not written down, take some time to seriously consider what your church values and make a list so future leaders will be able to execute the mission of the church based on its values. If you would like to see a copy of our church's mission and values, please feel free to visit our website at www. cowboyfellowship.org.

STRUCTURE

In 1 Corinthians 14:40, scripture says, *"But everything should be done in a fitting and orderly way."* As a leader, it is imperative that you not only understand the mission and values of your church, but you must understand its governing structure as well. How does your church function? Who makes what decisions? Where do you fit into the structure? These are all questions you must have the answers to if you are going to lead at a high level.

All churches have some sort of organizational structure. It does not matter how new, modern, big or small. Every church and every organization must have some structure and systems if it is to survive and thrive. Our God is a God of structure and order. Our universe is one of structure and order. It should come as no surprise to find that God's church has structure and order, too. To be the most effective leader possible, you must fully understand the organizational structure of your church. The leader must be ready and willing to work inside of the set structure. Should a leader choose to disregard the structure of the organization, the result is always the same: chaos and failure.

Too much structure can strangle an organization. Leaders must be careful to not over-organize and rob those they lead of the freedom that is necessary for life and success to thrive. Too many rules, papers to fill out and file, or people to report to will cause those you lead to quickly become frustrated. Therefore, balance is key to a healthy structure that helps instead of hinders an organization. With the proper balance, structure becomes something that empowers and strengthens an organization or ministry.

No matter how large or small your ministry or mission team, it is important that you have a clear and well-defined structure in place. This will help those you lead understand how your team will work. This will instill confidence in your team because structure takes out the guesswork. It also gives those you lead the confidence to make decisions and do ministry within the structure you have set up.

Finally, structure will give those you lead the ability to know where to go when they need help or when they need you to make a decision. Without a well-defined structure, your team will lack confidence, make decisions slowly, and suffer when things go wrong because they won't know who or where to turn for help. It is your job as a leader to develop some structure for your team that matches, complements, and agrees with the overall structure of your church. To achieve its fullest potential, your team must have at least a basic structure.

It would be impossible to explain the numerous types of structures at work in churches today. You will need to sit down with your pastor or leadership coach to find out exactly how your church is structured. Make sure that the structure in your team is similar to the structure of your church. As a leader you need to not only understand the structure of your church but you must operate within it as well.

CHAPTER SUMMARY

Understanding the overall mission, values and structure of your church will help you lead to your greatest potential within the Body of Christ. Leadership in the church, however, will be frustrating and full of failure if you fail to learn the mission, values and structure of your church. In order to lead and influence people around you, a leader must first understand the mission, value system, and structure of the organization.

Final Questions

1. Is it important to communicate the mission and values of the church to those you lead? Why or Why not?

2. Why is it not enough to just memorize the mission, values and structure of your church?

3. What are the values of your church? Why is it important to understand those values?

4. What is the overall mission of your church? How do the values of your church help achieve that mission?

5. What is the governing structure of your church?

6. Where do you fit into that structure?

7. As a leader, what are you authorized to do? What decisions can you make within the structure of your church?

8. In regards to your church structure who are you suppose to go to when you need help as a leader?

CHAPTER 4

—— Building a Team ——

Then the apostles and elders, with the whole church, decided to send men chosen from among them, Judas called Barsabbas and Silas, leaders among the brothers, to Antioch with Paul and Barnabas.—Acts 15:22 (NET)

I would not describe myself as a huge sports fan. I watch sports occasionally; however, I rarely have a single team in any sport that I rout for consistently. The only exception is basketball where I find myself always pulling for the San Antonio Spurs. I grew up near San Antonio and still live there today. My interest in the Spurs is much greater than the geography I share with the team, though. What I enjoy is watching them build a great team year after year.

Very few professional sports teams have been able to consistently have the caliber of teams that the Spurs have produced since the late 1990s. While the arrival of Tim Duncan was no doubt a major contributing factor, the real secret to their success has been consistently building a quality team around their franchise player. The Spurs' scouts and management always seem to find young, unknown, and undervalued players to turn into something more.

Even more amazing is the fact that the Spurs are always rebuilding because many of these young, unknown players become superstars, and thus are offered more money and better deals with other teams when their initial contracts expire. Being able to put together quality teams for five years is one thing, but they have done it for nearly two decades and achieved tremendous team success in the process.

Am I advocating that we build our teams the way the Spurs build their teams? Are we going to examine the Spurs' team building process? Absolutely not! I simply share this story to illustrate the power of an effective team that knows its mission and understands how its values and structure help it achieve the goal.

Every leader needs followers. If no one is following, you are not leading. These seem like obvious statements, but they lead us to some important questions. How do you build a team? How do you get people to follow you? Building a team is not easy and never will be, but building a successful team is rewarding. It does not matter if you are trying to build a successful sports team, a team at work or church, or a team for anything else in life; building a team will always have its trying and difficult moments.

Building a team takes time. It has taken years to build the team we have at our church, and we are still building. The team is not finished yet. Don't become frustrated if it takes time to build your team. Great teams take time to build. The cast is always changing. Older members move, join another team, or retire, and then new members come into the mix. You should never view your team as being finished or full. As a leader, you should always be scouting and building your team.

You will notice that the great leaders of the Bible all have certain things in common. Among those common traits, you will find that they were able to build teams of people. Paul, David, Nehemiah, Moses, Peter, and Jesus all built teams. Few leaders find themselves in a position where the team is already fully established and functioning at a high level. Even if you are taking over a team, it is likely that the team is incomplete or needs to be changed in some way to function better. As the leader of the team, you are expected to build and equip your team. This may mean that you enable others to help you scout, recruit and train. It may also mean that you do those things yourself. Either way, it is your responsibility to build a team.

——— THE MODEL ———

The model that will be presented to you in this chapter makes a major assumption. I am assuming that you have prayed about building your team. I am convinced that you can't build a great team without prayer. Since this seems to be an obvious point for Christian team building in the church, I will not spend much time on the topic and will assume that you are aware of the power of prayer.

The model to build a team is simple to outline and discuss on paper; however, be aware that the process is long and can be frustrating as you try to follow this model. This is not a new model but instead one that has been tried, tested and proven true for centuries. If you do these four steps, you will find that you will be much more successful in building a team.

The first thing you must do to build a team is *bring them in*. You have to find people to be on your team. You can't build a team without people. Yes, it's that simple. You must find them and bring them in. The natural question is, "How and where do I find them?" The "where" is simple. People all around you would love to be on your team. There is no shortage of people who would love to join you and help you fulfill the mission God has given your church, your team, and you. They are ready and willing to follow you, but how do you bring them in?

Most churches rely heavily on bulletin inserts, announcements from the pulpit, flyers, and newsletters to get the word out. While these methods may be somewhat effective, we have learned that there is a better and more effective way to bring people into and onto your team. It works well over 70%[5] of the time. It is much faster and much more effective than the traditional model. Are you ready to find out the secret? What we have found to work the best is a personal invitation.

Revolutionary, I know, but it works. If you want to bring people in, just ask people to join you! Tell them what you are doing and ask if they would like to be a part of it. In most cases, they will. Start

---

5   This is not a scientific number, just an estimation based on years of observation and experience.

with those you already know in the church. Then ask those you know outside of the church; then move on and make new friends and ask them, too. The best way to bring people in is simply to ask them. Good leaders understand the power of relationships and personal invitations.

You can't just walk up and say, "Hey, you wanna follow me?" That is not the way to bring people in. Bringing people in involves casting vision, sharing your ministry's mission, and being able to explain how your team helps fulfill God's mission for your church. People have to believe in you and in what you are doing. However, you have to know more than what you are doing. You need to know why you are doing it. As a leader, those you ask will want to see the passion and the vision you have for the ministry you lead. Be ready to answer their questions. Be ready to cast the vision and explain why this ministry or mission God has given you is important. Go out and ask them. It's the best way to bring them in.

The next step is *building them up*. Every strong leader knows you have to do more than just bring people in. You can't just bring them in and then stop. Imagine what our military would be like if they just brought people in, handed them some fatigues and an M-16, took down their cell phone number and said, "We will call you if we need you!" It would not work very well, would it? The Spurs are not consistently great only because they bring people in; they also develop individuals and build them up!

Basic training and pre-season workouts are about much more than getting the soldier or athlete in shape. It is also about building up their confidence levels. A leader will teach the new recruit that he or she can get over the obstacle, survive the long run in the heat or cold, and face any other challenge he or she might encounter. Leaders build team members up and help them learn to believe in themselves and their abilities. This is what you must do in the second stage of building a team: Build your people up and encourage them. Help them gain confidence and learn to believe in themselves.

This does not mean you lie to them or cheer them on for no reason at all. It does mean, though, that you celebrate every little success. You send them encouraging emails, cards, and drop a personal phone call in from time to time to tell them what a great job they are doing. You let them know how important they are and how excited you are that they are on your team. You build them up! You help them gain confidence in their areas of ministry. Once this has taken place, you move on to the third step in building a team. However, you never quit building people up.

The third step is *training* those you lead. Training is different than building. Building is about encouragement, and that should never stop. Training is about helping those you lead to learn skills they need to accomplish the ministry. Training is where you start to let those you lead do the ministry on their own. For example, you might have someone helping you in children's ministry or the nursery. You brought them in and asked them to help you with your class for a few weeks. During that time, you built them up and encouraged them; now it's time to train them.

In this part of the process, you might ask them to teach a lesson. You might say, "I will help you prepare and I will be here to assist you, but you are ready to teach the class yourself." You would then take the time to make sure that the person you are leading is trained and prepared when the day came to teach. Training is where you impart the skills and wisdom you have gained into those you lead so they can do the ministry. During this phase, you take a back seat and watch as God works through someone you have trained.

The final phase of this process is *sending them out*. You have brought them in, built them up, trained them, and now the time has come to send them out to do the ministry. Jesus did this with his own disciples and we must as well. Sending can take on many different forms. Someone may come into your ministry and be built up, trained, and then sent out to start or take over a different ministry. They might even leave and end up in a different church. Sending might also mean they become a co-leader or are able to do the ministry on their own.

For an example, let's stay with the previous illustration about children's church. You brought them in, built them up, and trained them. Sending might entail that person taking over the class entirely. It might mean that the individual is paired up with a newer member of the ministry team and assigned the responsibility to build, train and prepare to send that person now. Sending does not always involve losing the member of your team. However, it does always involve letting go.

Leaders are often fearful to send out those they have built and trained. This happens because, at this point, those being sent are really ready to lead. The leader will sometimes say, "What if they take my job?" or, "What if they take all of the things I have invested into their lives and leave to serve someplace else?" The answer is simple: find someone else to build, train and send. Continue to influence and lead through building and training. As a leader, your job is to influence, equip, and train those who follow you to do the ministry. Why did Jesus build, train and send those he brought in? He knew he would not be on the earth forever. Neither will you! Find them, build them, train them, and send them out.

It is important to note that these four steps we are discussing will most likely happen one-on-one between you and those you lead. In a church setting, you rarely get all of your volunteers in at the same time where you can build and train them all at once. Generally, you will have followers at all different levels of this process throughout your ministry. Use this process as a model for each individual that comes onto your team, not for the entire team as a whole.

——— **CHAPTER SUMMARY** ———

Building a healthy team of volunteers will be one of the most challenging things you do in church leadership. It will take time, patience, persistence, courage, wisdom, and much more. Don't become discouraged if your team does not grow as fast as you had hoped. Don't quit and give up when those you are leading fall away and leave for one reason or another. Just use this simple model to bring people in, build them up, train them, and finally send them out. Great leaders build great teams. Get started on yours today.

Final Questions

1.   Why is having a team important?

2. List some people you know who might want to be on your team. Set aside some time to call them or meet with them one-on-one this next week.

3. Write out the 4 steps in building a team in your own words.

4. Why do you think personal invitations work better than print and other traditional methods?

5. Explain in your own words what the difference is between the building and training phases.

6. What are some practical ways you can build others up?

7. Think about the ministry or mission God has called you to lead. List some specific things you will need to train others to do.

8. Why do you think it is important that we never stop building others up even after the training phase has started?

CHAPTER 5

————— Leading Change —————

For everything there is an appointed time, and an appropriate time for every activity on earth: A time to be born, and a time to die; a time to plant, and a time to uproot what was planted; A time to kill, and a time to heal; a time to break down, and a time to build up; A time to weep, and a time to laugh; a time to mourn, and a time to dance.—Ecclesiastes 3:1–4 (NET)

There may not be anything more daunting and dangerous than "leading change." It has been stated that there are three certainties in life: taxes, death, and change; and nobody cares for any of the three. As a leader, there will come a time when you identify the need for change in your ministry or church. Over time, God will clarify this need and prompt you to do something about the issue. As a leader, you have a few options:

The first is to pretend that the issue does not exist. You can be like many leaders before you and conclude that God was not talking to you or that the issue is not really that bad. You can ignore the signs, symptoms, and issues that are screaming change and refuse to address the issue.

Next, you can choose to acknowledge the need for change and perhaps even voice concern over the issues but fail to lead the change that is needed. Many leaders take this approach. They set out to explore what the cost and consequences of leading change might be, and when the resistance emerges, they cease their pursuit.

Finally, you can dare to lead the change that is needed. Leading change is: never easy, always costly, and incredibly dangerous. Whatever you are trying to change, you can be sure that some will not appreciate your efforts. Those who do not agree maybe be vocal, persistent, and passionate in their opposition. Others may silently slip out the back door, withhold their giving, or attempt to apply presure in other ways.

—— WHY CHANGE? ——

The normal reaction anytime anyone senses change coming is "why should we change?" Leaders generally sense the need for change and hear God's voice concerning change first. God will allow you to see things, sense things, hear things, and experience things long before others.

Consider Moses, one of the greatest leaders in scripture. As he walked out in front of the nation of Israel leading them toward the Promised Land, he was consistently leading the people to change. After all, there was much change that was needed with these people. They had been slaves, now they were free and their mindset needed to change. They had been Pharoah's property, then they became God's chosen people so their understanding of their purpose needed to change. The truth is almost everything needed to change in the lives of these people. As the leader, Moses was God's main instrument of change for this nation. As was the case with Moses, God still uses leaders in His church to institute change.

Those opposed to change will say, "but God never changes, so why are we changing?" They are right and wrong at the same time. While God does not change because He is perfect, we are constantly changing because we are not perfect. By refusing change we are claiming perfection and the reality is no person or church is perfect, so change will always be needed.

Things that are not changing are dying. That statement may be blunt, and a bit harsh but it is true. When anything in creation loses the ability to change, it dies. Your body is constantly in flux. The muscles, cells, chemicals, and even your blood is always changing. The air in your lungs is constantly being exchanged so that life can continue. When your body loses the ability to change, it dies. This principle is true of ministries and churches too.

Change is also a means of refreshment and vitality. Take a river that stops flowing for example. It is only a matter of hours, in many cases, before the bacteria, algae, and deadly microorganisms begin to thrive. What was once a source of pure, clean, refreshing water, quickly turns into a slimy, nasty, death sentence for those who drink from it. This radical transformation occurs for one reason, no change.

In his book *Autopsy of a Deceased Church,* Thom Rainer outlines twelve key issues that dying churches have in common. All twelve of these issues can really be summed up into one thing. They refused to change. Like everything else in life when churches stop changing they cease to possess real life, and will eventually die.

HOW TO LEAD CHANGE

As a leader, I am still learning about how to effectively lead change myself, however, I feel there are some simple and helpful tips that I can share with you. Every church is different and every situation requiring change is different. There are, some things that I have found to be helpful when it comes to leading change.

First, if at all possible, be very clear as to what and why God desires the change. It is unwise as a leader to attempt to lead change unless you have some level of understanding about the need for the change. Moses refused to accept the assignment to lead God's people from Egypt before God clarified the plan and gave assurances to Moses. Sometimes, we look at Moses and question his faith, but perhaps he was wise to ask for that clarification considering the magnitude of change that was about to occur.

Next, choose your words wisely. I have come to prefer the term transition over change for example. Transition seems to be more palatable by most people while still clearly indicating that a change is coming. Another term I have found to be helpful is progress. While people generally do not want to change, most people desire to see progress in their church. It is rarely wise to attempt sudden and dramatic change in church life anyway, so, when we attempt change we are actually leading people toward progress or making a transition.

Third, choose who you share with wisely. Many needed changes are killed before they ever have a chance to be implemented. Word gets out, the wrong people start to yell, and before you know it, the needed change is abandoned. When you sense God calling you as a leader to implement any kind of change, give the vision for that change time to grow and be clarified in your heart. Then prayerfully and selectively with God's help introduce the need for this change to others. When the time is right bring it to the masses.

Casting vision before, during, and after the change is important as well. If people forget the vision and purpose of your church or ministry and become focused on the change you are in for a rough ride. If, however, people remain focused on the vision and can see how the change enhances the purpose of your team, then leading any change will be much smoother.

If you are leading change, then you must be willing to change too. Frequently, in my personal experiences when leading change, God calls me to change as well. Generally this change occurs before I am prepared to lead others to adopt the needed changes. It is easy to become so excited about the change you sense is needed that you fail to realize that God desires to change something in you first.

Finally, choose your pace wisely when it comes to change. If you attempt to move too quickly, people will revolt. If you choose to move too slowly, people will abandon the process. Finding a pace that suits everyone is impossible but finding a speed that the majority can tolerate is the goal.

All transitions take time to implement. Generally speaking, the larger the change—the longer the transition will take. If you want to change the way the bulletins on Sunday are folded, a few weeks will likely be sufficient. If the needed change involves selling your current church property and relocating the entire campus, this change may take years or even an entire generation.

As leaders, we want change to happen quickly. Generally, we have seen the need, sensed the call, and been praying about the issue long before anyone else. As a result, when it is time to move; we are ready, willing, and excited. Others will not share your enthusiasm. As a result all change takes time. Sometimes God calls one leader to start the transition and then brings another to finish the job. Moses faithfully led God's people out of Egypt and through the wilderness, Joshua lead them into the land of promise.

WHAT IF THEY WON'T CHANGE?

If those you are leading absolutely refuse to change, what should you do? Again, this will vary from church to church and largely depend on the situation, however, there are some common points that can be made.

First, sincerely listen and attempt to understand why they are resistant to change. Do they have biblical or theological aversions to the change or is it personal preferences that are in the way? Good leaders are always listening to those they lead, yet they never let those they lead shout God down.

Next, change what you can, when you can. Most transitions take time and many come in phases. If your team is unwilling to implement everything; implement what they will accept as soon as possible. When they see positive things happening they will be more likely to support the other changes.

Pray for those you are leading. Again, I think of Moses, who on several occasions pleaded with God on behalf of the people he was leading. Despite their unwillingness to change and their poor treatment of Moses, he never stopped praying for those people. He never gave up on those people, and he never gave in and quit leading them toward change. Be the kind of leader that can stay the course with the people and the change.

Live the change before you lead the change. This is especially true if the resistance to change is strong. As the leader you must be living the change that you believe God wants to implement. It may be impossible to live that change fully without the buy-in of others but do your best to live it daily, in anyway possible. Many times people need to see the change before they will desire the change.

Finally, remember that loud does not equal large. Anytime there is change on the horizon those opposed to it may speak up. Some are opposed because it was not their idea. Others are opposed because the change will be uncomfortable. There will be others who just don't like you and, as a result, try to make your life difficult so they join the opponents to the change. In most cases, however, this is a very loud minority. Don't stop casting vision, following God, or give up on the change because of the noise a few people are making. If you stay with the transition process, you will lose some. If you decide not to change you will lose many more. After all this was God's idea in the first place, right?

―――― **CHAPTER SUMMARY** ――――

Change is never easy, and in ministry it is rarely a pain free experience. However, it is needed and vital to the health and life of all churches. When things stop changing they die. As a leader, you will be God's instrument of change in your ministry and church. Dare to live and lead the change God places on your heart.

Questions To Consider.

1.   Why do you think change is so hard for people? Why do you think we become more resistant to change as we get older?

2.   Why is change needed in the church? What happens if nothing changes?

3.   What are some of the common things you hear from people who are resistant to change?

4.   How will you deal with people who oppose change?

5. Have you seen any examples of churches that refused to change? What happened?

6. Why is understanding how to lead change important for leaders?

7. Why is it important to be patient when leading change?

8. Why do so many churches fail to change?

9. As a leader how can you best support your pastor during a time of transition in your church? Why is this important?

CHAPTER **6**

───── **Facing Problems** ─────────

For our struggle is not against flesh and blood, but against the rulers, against the powers, against the world rulers of this darkness, against the spiritual forces of evil in the heavens. For this reason, take up the full armor of God so that you may be able to stand your ground on the evil day, and having done everything, to stand.—Ephesians 6:12–13 (NET)

Every church has problems. As a leader, you will be confronted with problems more than the average attendee or regular church member. The greater your leadership role, the more problems you will face. For example, pastors will be asked to help solve more problems than a ministry team leader. A lay pastor, elder, or deacon will be asked to deal with more problems than the small group leader. However, the number of problems you face as a leader is far less important than the way you handle the problems. While all problems are different, most have several things in common and can be dealt with in similar ways. I believe there are five things a leader must do to effectively handle problems they encounter. Before we look at the method that a leader can use to solve problems, let's examine some of the different kinds of people you will encounter as a leader.

_____ PEOPLE YOU WILL MEET ON THE LEADERSHIP JOURNEY _____

Let's be honest; almost all of the problems leaders face in the context of church involve people. There is an old saying in church leadership circles that says, "The more people you have, the more problems you have." The overwhelming majority of people are not troublemakers, but the majority of people will at some point cause or be a part of causing a problem. Granted, many times this is unintentional, but, nevertheless, people and problems go hand in hand.

For example, Adam was close to his pastor and heavily involved in the church. He was on the leadership team and was known as a team player. Over the years, he had proven to be incredibly trust-worthy and competent as both a leader and friend. Adam took great pride and extreme ownership in both his ministry and his church, so when Jenny came to him and said, "I want to replace all of the vacuum cleaners for the children's department, but the children's minister told me we don't have enough money in the budget," Adam was puzzled. He was on the budget team at the church and knew that the children's budget had several thousand dollars in the account. He also knew that Jenny was right. The old vacuum cleaners needed to be replaced, and she was only asking for eight hundred dollars to purchase the new equipment. As the head of the budget team, he approved the purchase without checking with the children's minister. Two weeks later, he approved another purchase in a similar manner for over one thousand dollars.

The following month, Adam got a call from the children's minister who had received his monthly update on his budget in the staff meeting that day. The children's budget was $1,400 in the red because of Adam's good intentions. What Adam did not know was that the minister had recently bought VBS supplies and depleted the children's budget down to just a few hundred dollars. When the minister told Jenny there was not enough money in the budget, it was because he knew that there were some outstanding expenses that had not been added to the numbers on the budget. He had also explained to Jenny that the new vacuum cleaners could be ordered in a month or two once VBS was over, but Jenny, of course, failed to mention this to Adam. As a result of Adam's actions, he lost some influence with individuals in the church, and he caused some major budgeting problems for the children's minister.

This simple illustration is only one example of a kind of problem that is caused when well-intending people make assumptions or try to make a positive impact without fully understanding the situation. There are some in the church who will intentionally try and create problems. When they have a disagreement with the pastor, leader, or leadership team, they stand up and rock the boat. Some will even try to blow a hole in the ship to ensure that it sinks. Dealing with problems is just part of being a leader. Here are some types of people you will encounter as a leader while dealing with problems.

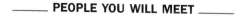

PEOPLE YOU WILL MEET

I call the first person the "poker." This person is someone that never really hurts you or causes big problems; instead, they are always starting little fires. They poke, pinch and irritate you on purpose. They use sarcasm and biting humor to try and mask comments that are intentionally meant to hurt and degrade you.

In grade school, I was told about "Chinese water torture." The idea was that some kind of device would be placed over your forehead, and it would slowly drip single drops of water down onto your brow right between your eyes. While a drop of water will not kill you, it will over time drive you insane! This is the goal of the poker; they pick, pinch, and poke in an effort to drive you crazy. To make matters worse these people will frequently use other people to do their dirty work.

So, how do you handle a poker? The best thing to do with a poker is confront him or her in a one-on-one setting. Pokers tend to be motivated by attention, and public confrontation generally makes you look worse than them. If you get so frustrated with them that in the middle of a team meeting you call them out, they will throw their hands in the air and say, "What are you talking about? I am just trying to help!" They play dumb and pretend to be as innocent as a dove. The others in the group will almost always look at you as if to say, "Wow, he is having a bad day. What's the big deal?"

The other members on your team have not felt or experienced the thousands of pokes and pinches that you have; therefore, your public frustration will seem unwarranted and too harsh. So, set aside some one-on-one time with the person. Let the individual know how you feel he or she is treating you with the constant barrage of pokes. The poker will likely deny any ill intent, but don't fall for this. They know exactly what they are doing. Be firm and let them know that you will not tolerate it any more, and you plan to document each instance and confront them each time they poke or pinch you. Every time they do it, confront them quickly and on the spot until they understand that their conduct will not be tolerated.

The next kind of person you will encounter is the "vine." This person tends to be very clingy. They will attach themselves to you and suck all of the life out of you if you let them. Sometimes a person will just look up to you so much as a leader that he or she always wants to be around you in a real effort to learn as much as possible. They may feel that they owe you because you helped lead them to the Lord or got them involved at the church. They want to help lighten your load, and they feel the only way they can do that is to attach themselves at your hip. If you perceive this to be the intent of the vine in your life, the solution is simple. Just be honest with them and talk to them about it. Give them some responsibility. Let them know that you will help them accomplish that task or ministry, but you want them to do it. Empower them, build them, train them, and then send them out.

If the vine is trying to form an unhealthy attachment, sometimes the person must be peeled away and removed. For example, Hannah was happily married to John. They had two kids and a good relationship. John had always been good to Hannah, but when it came to church, John was just not interested. So, Hannah came to church alone almost every Sunday. One Sunday, Hannah's "vine" arrived and approached her saying, "I would like to help on your team." Hannah was thrilled; after all, who does not want another volunteer? Over the next few weeks, Hannah started to notice that the vine was showing up to help her even on Sundays he was not scheduled to work. She started to suspect that this man, who was single, might have more than a ministry relationship in mind. Hannah started to talk about her husband and children more and more, and she started to try and distance herself from the vine. However, he always seemed to find his way to Hannah. She even thought about leaving the ministry and the church she loved so much because of this vine.

Hannah eventually, with the help of her pastor and others on the team, was able to peel the vine away. They both still attend the same church, but if Hannah had not been perceptive enough to recognize what was going on, the outcome could have been much different. If you feel that there is a vine attached to you with evil intent, you should tell someone you trust about it. Immediately seek help even if this vine is of the same sex and the issue is not romantic at all. Most of the time it will take more than one person to deal with a vine. Get advice and counsel from your pastor or someone else you know, and bring accountability and expertise to the table before the vine overwhelms you.

Every leader will eventually run into the "power player." The power player is someone who wants to run the show. They will generally try to do this in one of two ways. The first is publically and unashamedly. They will talk over you in meetings, cut your knees out from under you, organize and plan attacks against you, and try to destroy you in any other way possible. They are bullies! Most people know who these people are, but they still choose to side with them because they don't want to stand up against them. Others on your team might understand what is going on, but they are unlikely to help you deal with it. The power player is loud, mean, and down right ugly at times. Most people will not want to deal with them, especially if they are a public power player.

The second type of power player does the majority of their work in private. Many of the strategies are the same; they just don't have quite the boldness of the public power player. They tend to be more focused on strategy, and they are better long-range planners than the public power players. The public power player wants you gone today; the private power player just wants you gone. The funny thing about these types of people is that they don't usually want any responsibility. They don't want your job; in fact, these kinds of people generally do the most talking and the least work of any of the others. They just want someone they can control, manipulate, and use in your position.

Both the public and private power players can be dealt with the same way. You can let them run the show, which will work for a little while until their demands and control become so overwhelming that you quit, or you can stand up to them immediately. As soon as you identify power players, they must be confronted firmly and as fast as possible. Help them understand that, on your team, people who "talk" don't dictate the "work;" instead, people who "work" dictate the "talk." In other words, you can't just come in here and tell us how to do it; you need to earn your influence the same way everyone else does. Just because you are loud, rich, powerful, or successful does not mean you get to run the show. Those who are filled with the Spirit, not those filled with hot air, run the teams in churches. Typically power players will move on quickly once they perceive that they will not be able to dominate you, your team, or the church. The longer you put off dealing with power players, though, the harder it will be when you are forced to confront them.

The next kind of person you will encounter is what I call the "head nodder." They nod their heads up and down and agree with you in the meeting, but then they go out and do the opposite in practice. They are team players in the huddle, but when you say hut, they like to run their own plays. At first you might blame yourself for poor communication or think that they just did not understand, but as time goes on, the pattern will emerge. It will become clear that they just don't want to understand.

Andrew was a member of a team I led in college. He left every meeting with a smile on his face and in total agreement with the decisions our team had made. Sometimes his ideas were accepted and adopted just as he proposed them. Inevitably, though, within a few days or sometimes hours, I would hear through the grapevine that Andrew was upset and stirring things up behind the scenes. He was never happy! So, we would all meet again to calm Andrew down and come to another agreement. Again, everyone would leave smiling and in agreement only to find that in a short amount of time, our "head nodder," Andrew, was at it again. There may not be a more frustrating person to deal with than a head nodder.

The only thing you can do with a head nodder is communicate, communicate, communicate! Write things down. If your team makes a big decision that everyone needs to agree on, have the entire team sign a covenant on paper saying they made that decision. When you are in a meeting, go around the table and ask each person by name if they have anything else to add or say before you adjourn the meeting. Repeat your points and decisions over several times in several different ways so the final decision is very clear to everyone. Head nodders generally get the picture and are more reluctant to buck the system or decision if they feel like there is no way to "claim" they did not understand. When I started making audio recordings of our meetings and having the notes typed up and signed by everyone on our team before we left (all under the advice of my pastor), it was amazing to see how much Andrew changed. Our head nodder actually became a team player because he could no longer play the "I did not understand card" or the "he said, she said" game.

The "fluctuator" will cause many problems as well. This person needs constant love and attention. They always feel like they are mistreated and underappreciated. The world is always against them, and their deck of cards is always worse than everyone else's. These people tend to go from the highest part of life's mountains to the lowest valleys faster than anyone else. They can be your best friend and biggest fan on Monday and your worst enemy on Tuesday. They only remember the bad things, they choose to only see the here and now, and they fail to remember or recognize what happened yesterday. No amount of good things can ever make up for the one bad or negative thing that they perceive to be in front of them in that moment. Their emotional inconsistencies and personal unpredictability can cause huge problems for leaders.

When it comes to "fluctuators," encouragement, public recognition, and extreme patience are key. They need to be built up more than most, and whatever building you did yesterday needs to happen again today. Think of their encouragement as a sand castle on the seashore. You can work on it all day, build it up, and make it exactly the way you like it. Then, when you return the next day, it's all gone and the beach is exactly as it was when you found it the day before. While this may be somewhat of an over exaggeration, it's not far off.

These people need to be built up and recognized as much as possible. Highlight their efforts and achievements whenever it's possible. However, don't be surprised when they forget all about the nice things you said to them or about them yesterday. This is where the patience comes into play. When fluctuators get upset, remind them of how important they are to you and to God. Remind them about what you told them yesterday and about the great job they did last week. Remain calm; be patient and as gentle as possible when dealing with a fluctuator.

The final type of person I will mention is the "hard charger." This person is task oriented and very driven. He or she is focused and committed to results. They want to see it, touch it, smell it, hear it, and ultimately be able to brag about it. If eighty hours is what is needed, they are willing and they expect everyone else to be as well. They can be great team members or cause you a ton of problems, depending on how you deal with them. If they are not controlled, they can let their zeal, passion, and overall desires push others away.

Debbie was a "hard charger" on a team I once led. When Debbie joined the team, we had eleven other members. By the time I figured out how to handle Debbie, there were only four left. Debbie was a stay-at-home mother of one. She had lots of time and no other social or church commitments other than this one team. She was very passionate about the vision and mission of the team and church. Debbie committed twenty to thirty hours each week to this team, and she could not understand why others only gave two or three hours a week to such an important ministry. She would say things like, "I don't think you understand how important this is..." or "You are just not serious about this..." or "If you were really committed..."

These kinds of comments made others on the team feel less important, and, over time, she convinced other team members they were unworthy of serving in the church. Debbie did all of this in an effort to motivate and build the team, but her hard charging attitude caused many problems.

When it comes to dealing with hard chargers like Debbie, you must help them see the value of everyone and every minute that is given to the ministry. Remind them that God's call on their life is different from the call on someone else's life. You must also help them understand that tasks are less important than relationships. People like Debbie generally don't slow down enough to get to know other people because they are so worried about meeting a goal or deadline. Help them learn the value of relationships and getting to know other people on a deeper level.

When I was asked to lead another team, Debbie actually became the leader of the team she almost single handedly destroyed. With her help, we built that team back up to eleven people, and in the year after she took over as leader, the team grew to a total of eighteen people. The ministry actually multiplied.

None of these people are hopeless or useless in God's Kingdom. However, as a leader, you must be able to recognize them and know how you deal with them. Each of these types of people will cause different kinds of problems in your ministry. The sooner you can identify the type of person you are dealing with, the fewer problems you will face.

SO HOW DO WE DEAL WITH PROBLEMS?

The first thing a leader must do is *define the problem*. That means you must figure out what the actual problem entails. Problems are not always easy to define. Often times you will be presented with a problem only to learn that the root of the problem is not what you originally thought. It is important that as a leader, you do not jump to conclusions or make assumptions when faced with problems. Do your best to define the problem as accurately as possible. Ask questions to determine that you have a good understanding of the problem before proceeding on to the next step.

The common temptation here for all leaders is to assume you already completely understand the problem. To effectively solve problems, you must not rush through this initial step. It can take weeks to define the problem in some cases. If you start working on the issue before you really know what the problem is, you will likely be forced to start all over at some point down the road because you have been working to solve the wrong problem all along.

As a leader you must understand that the initial or stated problem is almost never the real problem. What I mean is that when someone tells you what there problem is don't automatically assume that the problem has been accurately defined. As a leader you should probe, pray, and attempt to discern if there is a deeper issue at work. Take whatever time is needed to define the problem. If you can't accurately define the problem you will never be able to resolve the problem.

After you define the problem, you can now start to *gather information* about the problem. You may need to talk to multiple people, you may need to do some research, you may need to get out the minutes from a meeting, or you may need to read an old email. Whatever it is, you want to gather the facts and obtain all the information possible in this second step. This process of gathering information may take minutes or weeks. Generally, the larger the problem, the longer it takes to define the problem and gather the necessary information. If you are dealing with a problem between two people, always gather information from both parties before making any statements or conclusions. Every problem has two sides, and the truth is usually someplace in the middle.

Once you feel you have all the information you need and the problem is well defined, you can *piece all of the facts and information you have together*. Keep an open mind during this process. Most times, you will end up pulling information from many different sources to get the full picture of the problem. Once you have pieced everything together, you are ready to do the last two steps to successfully solve a problem.

The fourth step is to *consider possible solutions*. Take some time to pray about and think through different solutions to the problem based on what you learned in the first part of this process. If you are able to talk about the problem with your team or other leaders, then take some time to brainstorm possible solutions together. If you are unable to talk to others due to confidentiality, then be sure you take the time to consider as many different solutions as possible. The worst thing you can do at this stage is to assume that your first solution is the best.

The final step is *picking the best solution and implementing it*. There is rarely a perfect solution to a problem, so you will be forced to pick the best solution available. If the problem was between two individuals, you will want to meet with both of them and explain the process you went through to determine the solution. Then, explain the solution in detail. If the problem is a church problem, such as how many restrooms to have in the new building or what to do with the budget surplus or shortfall, you will want to use the same process. However, have others help reinforce your solution to the problem. No matter what the problem is, if you take the time necessary in the first four steps of solving problems, you will generally end up with good results in the final step. Your problem will then be on its way to finding a true resolution.

THE WORST THING YOU CAN DO

When it comes to problems, the worst thing you can do is ignore the issue or delay dealing with it. Too many times this is exactly what we do as leaders. We hope and pray that the problem will solve itself. Leaders often refuse to get involved and just hope the problem goes away. For example, churches in decline often will not deal with the problem for years. Then they say things like, "We once had 500 people; now we only have 150. We have a problem and we need to do something." As you define the problem and get the facts, you will learn that they did have five hundred people *eighteen years* ago! Why did they not deal with the problem when attendance dropped to four hundred instead of waiting eighteen years? Since we don't like to deal with problems, we ignore them. Often times when we have problems with other people, we ignore the problem as well. There are thousands of examples of churches and church leadership teams splitting apart and being destroyed because of a small problem that was ignored. The worst thing you can do is ignore the problem.

Imagine for a moment you are a mariner on a nuclear submarine. You are on the first day of a 6-month mission, and while walking through the sub, you find a small water leak. What would you do? Would you ignore the problem or report it and get it fixed? Even a small leak can destroy a submarine if ignored long enough. You would not hope the leak would fix itself. You would not walk by and hope that someone else saw it and fixed it. You would jump into action. You would define the problem, get the information, put the information together, determine possible solutions, choose the best available solution and fix the leak. This is what we should do with the problems we face in our churches, on our leadership teams, and in our lives. Treat it as you would a water leak on a submarine.

CHAPTER SUMMARY

As a leader you will always have problems. Problems are produced by people, and leading people is what you have been called to do. Understanding the people you lead will help you identify the kinds of problems you are likely to face. Most problems can be solved quickly and painlessly if they are dealt with in a timely manner. As a leader, you need to be proactive in dealing with the problems that confront your life, ministry, and church. If you are not proactive, Satan will take small problems and sink your ship. Deal with the problem using the five-step model in this chapter, and you will find success in your area of leadership.

Final Questions

1. List and briefly describe the different types of people who may cause problems.
2. What is the best way to deal with each kind of person?
3. Which type of person are you or have you been?
4. Which of these people do you think you will struggle with the most? Why?
5. Why will all leaders be forced to help solve problems?
6. List the steps to solving problems and explain them in your own words.
7. Which of these steps will be the hardest for you? Why?
8. Why do we generally ignore problems?
9. As a leader, why must you be willing to confront problems?

CHAPTER **7**

_____SURVIVING A DROUGHT_____

I f you did not grow up on a working farm or ranch, it may be hard to understand the stress, pressure, and hardships that a drought can cause. Dry times bring about many hardships for those who depend on the rain for their livelihood. When the rain fails to fall from the sky it seems like everyone suffers. For some, the struggle is keeping the animals fed or crops alive while others deal with water restrictions that affect business and personal comfort. The bottom line is when it's dry everything is harder.

While every farmer and rancher in South Texas expects that the next drought will arrive soon, most church leaders operate under the assumption that they will always lead in a time of plenty. A leadership tenure generally starts off with high expectations and there is water and green grass everywhere. This generally does not last forever and there comes a time in every leader's ministry where the threat of drought becomes a reality. How you lead during the dry times is just as important as how you lead during the good times. If you have yet to experience a ministry drought, I pray the content of this chapter might be helpful to you when that time arrives.

There are several kinds of droughts that affect leaders. The first can be described as a spiritual drought. These times are marked by difficulty in hearing and understanding God. They may be filled with personal, financial, or moral failures. Sometimes we simply lose step with God and as a result find ourselves in a dry place, longing to live in the oasis of God's grace. I don't think I have ever known a single *honest* Christian who has never been through a dry, hard time spiritually. With that in mind, it should come as no surprise that most leaders will face this kind of drought at some point in their journey.

The second kind of drought is marked by a lack of help or poor volunteerism. There never seems to be enough help in ministry. Jesus said, *"The harvest is plentiful, but the workers are few."*[6] Leaders will sometimes experience adequate numbers of volunteers, but it is rare to have a true abundance. Eventually, all leaders find themselves in a time when there are not enough people to make the ministry work properly.

The temptation in this kind of drought is to do more of the work yourself as the leader. You put your head down and go to work, yet, this will work against you in the long run. The better option in a volunteer drought is to consolidate your volunteers in a wise way, and spend the bulk of your time recruiting new members to your team. It is difficult to allow the ministry to suffer while you build your team, but it is the best option for long term success.

The third thing that can happen is an idea drought where you run out of creative, fun, and interesting ideas for your team. You feel like you are just doing the same things you have always done and there is nothing new under the sun. This kind of drought can lead to frustration for both the leader and the team members.

You can also expect to face a budget drought at some point during your time as a leader. Like volunteers, there never seems to be enough money in church work to accomplish the mission. However, there are some seasons that are dryer than others. Leaders can quickly become discouraged when their budget is not increased or when it declines. When a needed piece of equipment or curriculum is not approved for purchase, it can quickly deflate a leader.

---

6   Matthew 9:37 (NET)

Almost all droughts lead to a decline in yield when it comes to fruit produced. While living through a drought, you generally see the overall fruit from your ministry decrease. This only adds to the discouragement and can destroy many leaders. Therefore, we should expect these things and be ready for them when they arrive.

THE GOOD NEWS

I can offer you some good news for a time of drought. First, all droughts end. Some last for weeks, or years, others for decades, or maybe even a generation, but eventually the drought will be over. Most droughts in ministry are short-lived, so press on and fight the good fight for the faith.

The next piece of good news is if you survive a drought, you will be stronger because of it. No matter what kind of drought it is, if you can live through it, your team and your church will thrive like it never has before. You will be wiser and better prepared for the next challenge that arrives.

Finally, remember that you are not in the drought alone. All churches and all leaders face droughts. If you are in a drought, the reality is others on your team or in your church are likely facing similar issues. Don't conceal your feelings in a drought. Open up to someone you trust, ask for prayer, seek guidance from others who have been through it before, and leave God room to work.

BREAKING A DROUGHT

I have found that there are three key ingredients to breaking a drought in your life. The first thing we must do to break a drought is seek the right source. When things get hard spiritually, financially, or in any other way it is critical that you continue to seek Christ. Resist the temptation to allow your flesh to rule. When we become dry we are quick to seek the wrong sources for refreshment. Your enemy knows that leaders are weaker during a drought and may present you with "wrong sources" that promise to quench your thirst. Be on guard for these attacks and know that there is only one who can satisfy your needs. His name is Jesus!

Next, saturate your spirit. When you are in a drought, saturate your soul with scripture. Spend extra time in prayer each day. Even if that time seems useless and it is difficult to remain focused, rest assured that God hears you, and in time will answer your cries for help. Don't neglect or stop going to church in a drought because this is when you need others the most. You need to surround yourself with other believers so that they can saturate you with spiritual encouragement.

Finally, sustain your service. When we are in a drought we often become convinced that our service to God is no longer needed, or appreciated, so we stop serving. Sometimes the leader will even conclude that the drought is a direct result of their service to God. They then drop out, make excuses and give up. This is never a good idea especially when you are in a dry time spiritually. Stay the course, continue to serve, and in time that service itself will bring refreshment to your soul. The other danger is that we work so hard trying to make it that we ignore the signs of burnout and blowouts. Sustain your service but be on guard against increasing it during a drought.

CHAPTER SUMMARY

All churches and all church leaders face droughts. These dry times are difficult, dangerous, and daunting for all leaders, but you can survive. If you are in a spiritual desert right now, rest assured all droughts come to an end. The rain will fall, and the rivers of God's mercy, grace, and blessings will flow soon. Until then, seek Christ, saturate your spirit, and sustain your service.

Questions To Consider

1. Why is being prepared for a drought important for all leaders?

2. How do you survive a drought?

3. Have you ever been through a dry time spiritually? What did you learn during that time?

4. When you are in a leadership drought who can you talk to in your church?

5. Why is seeking the right source critical during a drought?

6. How long do droughts last? Why is knowing this important?

7. Who can you think of in the Bible that went through a drought? What can you learn from their journey?

CHAPTER 8

———— Burnouts & Blowouts ————

When I turned sixteen, I took the driving test, received my license, and bought my first vehicle. The thrill of being able to drive wherever I wanted after school was exhilarating and sufficient. However, not many weeks passed until driving was not exciting enough anymore. I started doing burnouts and other unwise things while driving. Within a matter of weeks, my tires were ruined and I was forced to buy a new set with my own cash. This was an expensive and important lesson in my life. You can squeal the tires and have fun for a moment, but it won't be long until they are burned out.

With two decades of ministry under my belt, I can honestly say that burnouts and blowouts are the two reasons most leaders leave ministry. This happens at all levels in church from the pulpit to the pews. What makes this even worse is that both burnouts and blowouts are totally preventable. If you want to have a long, effective, and fruitful tenure as a leader then you need to pay careful attention to this chapter.

_____ BURNOUT [7] _____

When the Apostle Paul was writing to the workers of the churches in Galatia he stated, _"So we must not grow weary in doing good, for in due time we will reap, if we do not give up. So then, whenever we have an opportunity, let us do good to all people, and especially to those who belong to the family of faith._[8] Isn't it interesting that he feels it necessary to warn Christian workers about becoming weary doing good things? Today, we often call growing weary in ministry—burnout.

Well, you say, "I'm not in the ministry". Yes, you are, if you work in the ministry of a local church in any capacity. You are in ministry if you are part of a leadership team, an elder, a lay pastor, a team leader, a Bible study leader, a children's worker, a band member, or any of the necessary persons it takes to enable a church to fulfill its mission. You may not be in vocational ministry, but you are in the ministry.

It has been said of evangelical churches that, "When they find a good horse, they will ride it until it drops". That's just another way of saying that church needs are such that when a volunteer is found, who can and will do a good job, they just keep giving them things to do. And, unless the volunteer takes great care, overuse becomes burnout, and we become weary in our well doing.

What is ministry burnout and what causes it? One of the best explanations I've seen declares that, "Burnout is the result of prolonged stress, overextension, and hurriedness. The nervous system gets stretched until it loses its resilience and renewal capacity. It becomes more difficult to snap back from hard work, to 'get up' for challenges, and to adequately rest". You're tired all the time even though you haven't done much of anything. You feel like withdrawing, even from activities you truly enjoy. Before long you start to feel worthless. In this brief explanation about burnout, there are several characteristics to be aware of.

---

7   My friend Sunny Spurger, who has granted me permission to share this information with you, wrote this section on burnout in the 1st edition of Dare to Lead. Much of this section remains the same in the 2nd edition however I have added additional info that I have learned about burnout as well as additional scriptures to reinforce the points in this section. Finally I added a section on blowouts at the end of this chapter.

8   Galatians 6:9–10 (NET)

PROLONGED STRESS

Contrary to popular belief, stress is not something that happens to us. Stress is how we respond to what happens to us. Stress is not so much an action as it is a reaction. This is the precise reason why some circumstances don't bother us much at all while others may cause us a great deal of anxiety or stress. It's not what is happening that matters as much as how we respond to what is happening. This characteristic of burnout occurs when certain things continue to happen to us, but there is no end in sight and we don't respond well. It seems as if there is no relief. Over time, this pressure increases to the point where burnout is the end result.

OVER EXTENSION

This is when we allow ourselves, or others, to put too many things on our plate. Each of us has only so many emotional dollars to spend in any given day. When the demands on our emotional reserve are depleted, and then more demands are made, we are overextended and in danger of burning ourselves out. Time is the most important element in our lives we tend to overextend. Because there are only a limited number of hours in any given day, and a limited number of days in our lifetime, we are tempted to overextend ourselves in an effort to do more good. In the process we generally do a great deal of harm instead. There has to be a balance between the personal time with God, family, work, rest, play, self-care, and the ministry.

HURRIEDNESS

Ministry often has a sense of urgency attached to it. It is difficult to say to those in need, "I can't come right now. Can this wait?" As leaders we seem to be running constantly from one crisis to the next, from one meeting to the next. The more we are asked to do, the faster the world turns. Ministry is a very important and eternally significant task and thus we should work at it with all of our hearts. Hurriedness, however, can damage our heart for service in the long run if we don't slow down to enjoy the fruits of our labor.

SIGNS OF BURNOUT

When stress continues and we become overextended in our commitments and everything seems to need an immediate response from us, we begin to experience some of the following symptoms of burnout. Recognizing these in ourselves or in the members of our team will help us identify the onset of burnout and defeat it before it destroys us.

Sapping of Nervous System. There may be an awareness that a normal sense of self-control is lacking. A person may become more irritable, short tempered, impatient, and critical than is usually observed by those around them. Things that would not bother them usually may now draw a heated or illogical response.

Inability to Face Challenges. Most folks are in a given leadership position because they have been seen as someone who can get a certain type of job done. For the most part, they have been successful in meeting these expectations, but as the weariness of pressure and the constant demands of their ministries continue, they find that they cannot do what they once could and indeed often don't want to do their assigned task. They simply do not want one more expectation to be placed on them.

Inadequate Rest. Many who experience burnout are what some would call "hard drivers". If something is not going well they feel that throwing a few more hours at it will get the job done. This approach often makes it difficult for them to stop to be refreshed or to turn off at night so that they can sleep. Most health studies show that the average person needs at least eight hours of sleep each night. Most people in America do not get this much sleep, and in the grip of burnout they get even less. Sleep deprivation takes a terrible toll on health, mental alertness, and overall effectiveness. So, we sleep less to get more done and end up doing a much poorer job at the things we need to do well.

Withdrawal. As the symptoms discussed above increase, the person moving into burnout increasingly withdraws from their relationships and responsibilities. They realize that things are not going well and they don't want to talk about it, don't want it to be pointed out to them, and certainly don't want to have any more given to them. This move into withdrawal can be indicative of situational depression.

Feelings of Worthlessness. The result of the characteristics and symptoms identified with burnout is often a feeling that the person is not worthy to have been put in this position in the first place. They feel that they have failed their church, failed those who asked them to serve in the respective ministry, and have ultimately failed God. This is especially true for those who have come to identify themselves with the role of their ministry. They may not want to serve anymore in this ministry or any other. In many cases the guilt associated with burnout will cause them to leave the church.

Roy Oswald has developed a description of a burnout cycle for those in the ministry. In it he depicts the stages of an emotional journey for those in Christian service.

 **STAGES OF BURNOUT**

Stage I: The person is excited about the call extended to them to serve God and the church. There is a strong commitment to serve to the best of their ability. There are high ideals and wonderful expectations.

Stage II: Soon they begin to realize that there are too many people to serve. There is a feeling of being surrounded by a sea of human need and crises that seem to never end.

Stage III: In trying to meet all the needs, they see that they become physically exhausted and abuse their body with the lack of sleep, lack of healthy activity, and fast eating. This abuse places a great strain on their family, their marriage, and their other relationships. They become frustrated as they struggle with living out their convictions about their ministry and service.

Stage IV: There is a growing sense of helplessness, hopelessness, and powerlessness. It is as if they feel trapped. A quiet internalized despair sets in as there is a growing desire for privacy.

Stage V: The minister/volunteer begins to resent the people they have been called to serve. Their responses to others become snappy and sharp. They use sarcasm and biting humor when dealing with others.

Stage VI: There comes feelings of guilt and shame for the fact that, "I responded to this call in order to serve people and now I resent them. In truth, I don't even enjoy being around them."

Stage VII: The cycle comes full circle. The minister has a resurgence of zeal or a rededication to try even harder than ever. They throw themselves into the ministry with greater passion rather than backing away for replenishment and discernment.

THE PROPER RESPONSE

Jesus knew about the threat of burnout for His disciples. In Matthew 11:28-30, He said to them, *"Come to me, all you who are weary and burdened, and I will give you rest. Take my yoke on you and learn from me, because I am gentle and humble in heart, and you will find rest for your souls. For my yoke is easy to bear, and my load is not hard to carry."* [9] We know that Jesus valued rest and frequently retreated by himself or with a small group to be refreshed (Read Matthew 14:23, Luke 5:15-16 and Mark 1:32-33, 35). Burnout is not a new issue for church leaders, it is something that has always been a temptation and struggle for those in ministry. You are not the first to experience it, so take heart and then take a break.

---

9   Matthew 11:28–30 (NET)

If you are going to last for the long haul in church leadership, you must be able to identify the signs of burnout and exercise the discipline to confront this leader killer immediately in your life. Rest, relaxation, reflection, and some extended prayer times will help. But ultimately, there needs to be a more consistent focus for all leaders to avoid burnout.

Greg Baird wrote an article in 2005 titled, "Burnout Proof Your Ministry". In the article, he suggested that instead of getting "**burned out**", we need to stay "**F.I.R.E.D. U.P.**" in our ministries. He offered seven ways to do this:

F—Focus on Relationships

In truth, ministry is all about relationships. It's about our relationship with God, the people we are serving, the other ministers we work with, and our families.

I—Identify your calling

Why are you doing what you are doing? Is it because it's something God has given you to do or simply because you are filling a spot that needed a warm body in it?

R—Recognize your gifts, abilities, and limitations

Do you know what your spiritual gifts are? Are you working/ministering in an area that best utilizes your gifts and abilities? Are you serving in an area that does not bring you joy or produce fruit for the Kingdom?

E—Exercise your mind and body

In the Hebraic understanding of the makeup of man, we are mental, emotional, physical, and spiritual. We are all four all of the time. Each one affects the other. When we neglect to keep any one of these areas sharp, strong and growing, we diminish the contributions of the other three.

D—Develop your ministry skills

Continuing to grow in the development of your ministry skills is really not an option. None of us is ever as equipped as we need to be. Working in an area where you are not sure what you are doing is the surest way to become frustrated. We work harder at it with less and less success.

U—Understand the place of your ministry

Your ministry has an important place in your life, but it is not your only responsibility. There is a vital need for balance in the areas of worship, work, rest, and play. Keep your ministry in its proper place and balance.

P—Pray

When Jesus "got away from it all", what did He do? Most often He got away to pray. Without this essential tool for two-way communication that God has given us, we lose our direction, our security, and our instruction for the task of the ministry.

BLOWOUTS

Blowouts are less common than burnouts in the ministry, but they still happen far too frequently. A blowout occurs on a tire for several main reasons. The first is overloading. If you put more weight on a tire than it is rated to hold you are asking for a blowout. Tires also blowout when there is a weak spot or a blemish of some kind that is present in the rubber. Sometimes this blemish is detectable, but many times it is not. The final cause for blowouts is a catastrophic event such as running over a large object on the road. Surprisingly, these same issues are what lead to blowouts in the lives of God's leaders as well.

What is a ministry blowout? Well, they come in all shapes and sizes, but they are almost always painful experiences for all involved. A blowout occurs when a leader (generally after being burnt out) blows up and abandons the ministry, and the church. Many times they leave their faith altogether. Blowouts are bad for the leader and the church as a whole. They make lots of noise, and cause a great deal of pain and confusion for all involved. So, why do they happen?

Ministry blowouts occur for several reasons, the first is overload. Overload generally leads to burnout, however, some leaders hang on and continue to pile even more on until the blowout occurs. What most ministry leaders fail to realize is that ministry can't be separated from the weight we carry in other parts of our lives as well.

When you add the combined weight of work, family, community involvement, social responsibilities, and other normal activities with the weight of the ministry it can become too much. Things frequently change in our lives as well. When a work schedule changes it can add weight, when the family environment is unhealthy, extra weight is added. Eventually you just can't bear the weight anymore. When this happens, a blowout occurs, and sadly many blame the church, pastor, or ministry for the problem and leave. The reality is that most of the weight we carry in life has very little to do with ministry. Learning to examine your load and being diligent to unload things before taking on additional weight is important to avoid blowouts.

The second cause of leadership blowouts is weak spots or blemishes in the leader's character. While these kinds of blowouts happen, they are less common than the overload blowouts that we previously discussed. However, as our leadership responsibilities grow, there are frequently unknown blemishes that surface. Most leaders deal with these, but some refuse to work on their weak spots and it eventually leads to a blowout.

Finally, there is the catastrophic event. This can be anything that shatters a leader's world. The loss of a spouse or child, for example, can cause a blowout. When the senior pastor resigns or leaves to serve in another church, leaders will sometimes blowout. A major church transition such as moving locations, building a new facility, or major ministry expansion can cause blowouts as well.

Burnout and blowouts are difficult to spot in our own lives. Therefore, it is imperative that we help each other in identifying these leadership killers before they have their full effect in our lives. If you sense burnout or see blowout potential in the life of another leader, lovingly attempt to help them. If you see it in your own life, ask your pastor or another leader to help you deal with the issues before they destroy your ministry. Always be on guard against burnouts and blowouts, check your ministry tires frequently!

CHAPTER SUMMARY

Burnouts and blowouts are preventable. Leaders must constantly be evaluating their own lives and the lives of those they lead for signs indicating a burnout or blowout is coming. Take the time to rest, relax, and refresh when you feel the stress and pressure of ministry becoming overwhelming. Burnouts and blowouts are never beneficial therefore they should be avoided at all costs.

Final Questions

1. Can you list the three characteristics related to burnout?
2. Which of them do you most identify with? And, why?
3. Has burnout been a problem for you in the past?
4. Have you seen a burnout affect someone else? How?
5. Who can you talk to when you feel burnout starting to take over in your life?
6. Do you believe that burnout is real in ministry?
7. List some signs or warnings of burnout.
8. List some of the things that can help us avoid burnout.
9. Have you ever seen a ministry blowout? What was the cause?
10. How do you think blowouts can be prevented?
11. What stage of burnout are you in right now?

CHAPTER **9**

_____ **WHEN IT'S TIME TO LEAVE** _____

Genesis 12:1–2 (NET)—¹Now the Lord said to Abram, "Go
out from your country, your relatives, and your father's house-
hold to the land that I will show you. ²Then I will make you
into a great nation, and I will bless you, and I will make your
name great, so that you will exemplify divine blessing.

You might be thinking, "I am just getting started as a leader, why are you going to talk to me about leaving?" The reason is because there comes a time in the lives of all leaders when it is time to leave, and how you leave is as important as how you lead.

I have seen a large number of faithful and successful leaders leave in hurtful, wrong, and unbiblical ways over the years. When this happens, it always negatively affects the church, and it can also cause people to view the leader in a poor light. More importantly, it can cause non-believers to view God and His church in a negative way when they witness a leader leave in the wrong manner.

Why you leave is less important than how you leave. Everyone leaves at some point. Some leaders burnout, others blowout, some move, and others will feel called to a different aspect of ministry. There is retirement for some, and God-ordained extended sabbaticals for others. Ultimately, there comes the time when all leaders leave earth and transition into eternity. Whatever the reason, all leaders leave. So it is important that when the time comes we leave well.

89

——— WHEN TO LEAVE ———

I must be honest and confess that I have only left four ministry positions in my career to date. The first was a summer youth intern position that I left because the summer was over. Two of the other positions were at churches where I was interim pastor, and my time came to an end naturally when the church found the person they were looking for to lead their congregations. The fourth was a position I had at the Baptist Student Ministries on the Texas State University campus where once again, my departure was not necessarily of my choosing, but rather my two year term in that role expired. In May of 2003 my role at the BSM ended and the church I pastor to this date started, so to be honest I have never really left a ministry. So how can I even write this chapter? Unfortunately, I have had the chance to observe many leaders leave over the years and have made note of those who left well and those who did not, and I hope to share those lessons in the pages that follow.

Knowing when to leave is the most logical place to start this discussion. Discerning God's will in leaving is an extremely delicate process that requires a great deal of faith. While there are no absolutes, I do believe that there are a few words of wisdom I can share with you when it comes to knowing when it is time to leave.

First, you should never leave during a drought. There is an entire chapter in this book dedicated to surviving a drought because all leaders face dry, difficult, and challenging times in ministry. It's during these times that we are tempted to look at the greener grass on the other side of the fence and contemplate leaving our position as a leader. I have known many leaders who left in a dry time in their ministry only to find that the green grass on the other side of the fence was just a mirage and the drought followed them to their new position. You don't outrun a drought, you survive it, so never leave just because your ministry is going through a drought.

Next, you should not leave because you are angry or upset. There will always be disagreements in ministry, and unfortunately this is when many leaders jump ship. Rather than working through the difficult times, they decide to leave instead. The problem is they almost always regret leaving. Furthermore, their anger almost always causes them to leave poorly. If you become upset and are thinking about leaving, take time to pray about it first. Let the situation cool off, work the problem out, then after the problem has been settled, if you still feel leaving is best, make your final decision. In so doing you leave behind a healthy ministry, healthy relationship, and a healthy leadership legacy. Many times after the problem is resolved the temptation to leave subsides.

Finally, you should not leave unless there is a strong, Godly, capable leader ready to take over your ministry. God rarely calls someone to abandon a ministry that is important to His Kingdom without first revealing who the next leader is going to be. If there is no one that can fill your role, and if you feel like God wants your ministry to continue, then you can be certain it is not your time to leave.

HOW TO LEAVE

I have always found it interesting that when leaders leave in the Bible they rarely do so suddenly. There is frequently a process and time for leadership transition that takes place in scripture. Consider Moses and Joshua or David's rise to power. We see it in the New Testament church and in the life of Jesus. Christ did not just leave, rather He gave lots of clues and direct warnings to what was about to happen. He came back to help the Apostles make the transition, and He assured them that the Holy Spirit would never leave them. Their leader, Jesus, was replaced by the Holy Spirit in a logical manner.

This rarely happens in churches, however. Generally the pastor just gets up one Sunday and says "Well, I am leaving because God has called me to go..." Or the lay leader sends an email or text saying , "I quit," or "I can't do this anymore." Sometimes people stop showing up all together and don't even take the time to explain why. When it is time for you to leave, so far as it depends on you, don't leave suddenly.

Next, leave in an open and honest manner. Don't say, "Well I am stepping down from leadership, but I am still going to come to church here," then never show up at church again. Don't say, "I am not mad about anything. God just told me this is the right time to leave," and then go into the community and be mad about something. If there is a problem and you have attempted to work it out with your pastor and elders, and no solution could be achieved, you can honestly say, "I am leaving because there were some issues we could not work out." Always be honest with people as to why you are leaving and what your intentions are after you leave.

When you leave, don't make people pick sides. If you are leaving in a manner where you are asking people to choose between you and the church or ministry team then you can be sure you are leaving in the wrong way. Leaders are people who have influence, and if you use that influence to split, dismantle, or attempt to destroy the bride of Christ (the church), you might want to consider who the groom is. If your departure is one that creates a desire to take other people with you, then you should be extremely careful and cautious as to what your motives are in leaving.

You should do everything in your power to leave on a positive note. Encourage those who are staying behind on the team. Endorse the new leader and extend whatever influence you have to helping them get off to a great start. Let everyone know that you will be praying for them, pulling for them, and ready to serve them in any way you can. Then follow through with those things.

When you leave, stay involved in your church. Show up on Sunday, participate in some way in the life of the church as a whole. Leadership is tough, and I am convinced that there are certain seasons where God calls us to lead and others where He allows his leaders to rest and refresh through service. Just because you are not leading does not mean you have permission to disappear, so stay involved, and be a part of the Body of Christ.

THE DIFFICULTIES YOU MAY FACE

The longer you serve and the higher the capacity of your leadership, the more difficult leaving well becomes. It is also true that the longer you serve and the higher the capacity of your leadership, the more important leaving well becomes. There are several things that I have witnessed leaders face upon leaving their leadership roles. These things occur in the lives of those who leave on both good and bad terms. They occur in the life of both the professional and lay minister, so be prepared to face these challenges as you attempt to leave well.

The first is what I call the loss of knowledge. As a leader, you tend to have a great deal of knowledge about what is happening in the life of the church. You attend meetings that others don't. You hear about new programs first. You are asked to pray about problems that many never know exist. The greater your leadership role, the more things you tend to know. pastors generally have more ministry knowledge than elders. elders more than team leaders, team leaders more than co-leaders, and so on.

Once you leave there is a loss of knowledge that takes place over time. You are no longer in the loop when decisions are made, and you naturally have less knowledge about why things are being done the way they are. This can be extremely difficult if you are accustomed to being in the conversation. Equally difficult is giving the remaining leadership the benefit of the doubt and being able to realize that they are making decisions based on current knowledge, not the older knowledge you possess.

Next, there is a loss of influence. Like the loss of knowledge, this influence fades over time. The longer you have served and the capacity in which you served will dictate how quickly your influence erodes. As a leader, people frequently ask you questions, seek out your opinion, or want you to get behind their idea. The reason this happens is because as a leader you have influence. When you leave, your level of influence changes. This can be a difficult transition for some leaders.

There is also a loss of relationship that takes place when you leave a leadership role. This happens primarily with the church staff, but can occur with other leaders as well. As a leader in your church you tend to have more access to the staff at your church. You see each other at meetings, talk on the phone, communicate through email, and spend large amounts of time together doing ministry. When you leave, these things decrease. Your ministers still love you and care deeply for you, but there will be a new leader in your position that your pastor is trying to connect and communicate with. Over time your relationships will change. The temptation is to think that it's because people don't care about you anymore, or that you were just being used while serving in your leadership role. The truth is that relationships among active leaders are just different. They are not better or worse, just different. Over time you will adjust to the new pace of your relationships.

Finally, there is a loss of control. As a leader in the church, you help make decisions, set policy, and cast votes to adopt various things. It is easy to become used to these roles as a committee chair or team leader. When you are no longer leading your team and realize that you have less control in the direction of the church, it can be a difficult thing to accept.

CHAPTER SUMMARY

Leaving is never easy and is rarely without hardship and pain. Saying goodbye for any reason is difficult, but you can do certain things to make the process better for yourself and God's church. Although you are just now starting your journey as a leader, the day will come when it is time to leave. I hope that when that day arrives you will pick up this book and review the principles outlined in this chapter.

Questions To Consider

1. What did you think about the statement, "how you leave is as important as how you lead." Do you think that is true? Why or why not?

2. Have you ever seen a great leader leave poorly? What kind of impression did that leave with people?

3. Why do you think it is important not to leave during a drought, period of frustration or anger, or without a capable co-leader in place?

4. Why do you think it is so hard to leave well?

5. Can you think of some leaders in the Bible who left well? What can they teach you about leaving?

6. Why do you think it is important for leaders to remain faithful in church, even after they leave their leadership position?

CHAPTER 10

Unity

How good and pleasant it is when brothers live together in unity!—**Psalms 133:1**

When you hear the word UNITY what do you think of? You might think of a strong marriage or a successful sports team. We all think of different things when we hear this word. When I hear the word "unity", one word always comes to mind—SPARTA! You might be familiar with the movie *300* that depicted the Spartan warriors' ability to fight as a unit in the battle of Thermopile. Three hundred men held the largest, most powerful army the world had ever known at bay for days. This was possible for one reason; they knew how to fight as a unit. They were unified in every move, and every thrust of the spear. They were a unit in all they did. This unity did not come easy for the Spartans.

Spartan boys were taken from their parents at age 7 and placed into military training. They were placed in barracks with other boys their age. Those boys would be the men they would fight with until age 60 when they were allowed to retire. They learned to love each other. They cared for each other's wounds, they worked together, and they trained together so that each warrior knew what the others were doing. They trained constantly with the same group of young boys who became teenagers and men together.

At around age 13, the boys were taken from their barracks and given one pair of clothes. They had no shoes and no food. For an entire year, the boys had to survive in the open wilderness as a unit. If they survived this year (and many did not) they would continue their training. Then at around age 20, they were given their first official military orders and saw combat.

It was not until age 30 that the men were considered worthy to marry, reproduce, and live away from their barracks. Those who were still living at this point had spent 23 years with their brothers in arms. It created a unified fighting force, the likes of which has never been reproduced. These men would often go home only to work the fields, reproduce, and make sure things were in order. They would then return to their fighting units to train and live with their comrades.

The Spartans were known around the world to be one of the deadliest and most effective fighting forces. Sparta was not a big country, but it was indeed a country with a big reputation, and no one wanted to mess with the Spartans if it was avoidable. For leadership purposes, the Spartans teach us two things about unity.

The first is that achieving unity is not easy and does not happen quickly. As we will learn later, our unity comes from and through our Lord Jesus Christ, so in a sense it has already been achieved for us. This true and easy unity can only be found in a perfect world void of sin. As a leader, the world in which you operate is far from perfect. It is full of people who become prideful, jealous, and vicious at times. Those you lead will gossip, bite, and hurt you many times on purpose. The sinful world in which we live as God's leaders makes unity difficult at best, and next to impossible at worst. Like the Spartans, we will have to work hard and for many days, weeks, months, and years to become a people who can operate in total unity. It is hard, very time consuming, and requires work.

The second thing the Spartans teach us is that unity is more than a word or an idea. Unity is a tool and a mighty force that God can use if we do the work and take the time to achieve it in His church. We will never know how many Kings and kingdoms thought of invading Sparta and chose to abandon their plans simply because of the unity in the Spartan army. You see, once real unity has been achieved often times unity in and of itself will be enough to ward of the enemy from launching his attack. If your team or church is unified, the enemy will turn his sights and attention to a weaker and less unified group. A unified church is difficult to defeat. So how important is unity in God's church? I would say it's one of the most important things a church or team can have.

THE SOURCE OF UNITY

Ask a thousand different people what the job of a pastor is and you will get a thousand different answers. Some will tell you the pastor's or leader's job is primarily made up of things like: hospital and nursing home visits, praying for the sick, ministering to hurt families, doing mission work, running the administration of the church, keeping the church clean and the grass mowed, being involved in the community, preaching on Sunday, and the list could go on and on and on. Pastors and leaders will be called upon to do many, if not all of these things. However, the biblical job description for leaders in the church is found in the book of Ephesians. This chapter of Ephesians is really a chapter about unity as well.

The chapter begins with a call for unity among the believers and the Apostle explains why unity is possible in the church.

> Ephesians 4:1–6 (NET)—*1I, therefore, the prisoner for the Lord, urge you to live worthily of the calling with which you have been called,2 with all humility and gentleness, with patience, bearing with one another in love, 3making every effort to keep the unity of the Spirit in the bond of peace. 4There is one body and one Spirit, just as you too were called to the one hope of your calling, 5one Lord, one faith, one baptism, 6one God and Father of all, who is over all and through all and in all.*

We can all agree that trying to get unity in a small family unit is hard enough. Trying to achieve unity on your committee at work or on a team at church can at times seem impossible. So how can we then expect to have unity as a church body? In essence, our goal is not so much to create or manufacture unity, but instead the Apostle says it is to keep or some translations say "maintain" unity. While the Spartans had to create and maintain unity, Christians must only maintain it since God, Himself, creates it. We are not unified under a church name, Pastor's vision, denominational lines, or the church constitution. Our unity is in Jesus Christ, the KING OF KINGS and LORD OF LORDS! Therefore, we are to make every effort to keep the unity of the Spirit through the bond of peace.

This is all possible because we are already one body; we have one Spirit, one hope, one Lord, one Faith, one baptism, and one God who is over everything. Our unity as a Body of believers comes not from ourselves but from being one with the God of the universe. God has unified us through his one and only Son, Jesus Christ. Our goal is to keep and maintain the unity that we already have in Jesus.

In a perfect world without sin, unity would be easy because we would all have and keep our focus on Jesus, the author and perfecter of our faith. This is why in heaven we will all live in perfect unity, for our whole and total focus shall be on the Father, Son, and Spirit. For now though, we must attempt to lead in the world in which we live. In this world, selfishness, pride, greed, hate, anger, and temptation to push others down in order to pull ourselves up rules. So what is a leader to do?

THE NEED TO FOCUS

If you want to keep the unity you have to increase your leadership to another level. In doing so, you must make Christ the focus of two things. The first is your life! Jesus can be the focus of nothing else until He becomes the focus of your life. As a leader this is critical, and without it, unity will evade you all of your days. Not only at church, but at home, work, in the community, and every other place. Jesus must become your all-consuming focus in every decision, action, and desire that you have. For this is the greatest commandment of all.

Matthew 22:36–37 (NET)—[36]*"Teacher, which command-ment in the law is the greatest?"* [37]*Jesus said to him, "'Love the Lord your God with all your heart, with all your soul, and with all your mind.'*

Once you have made Jesus the focus of your life, you must make Him the focus of your group or team. It seems strange to even have to say this, but how many churches and ministries have been destroyed because Jesus was not the focus? How many church splits have had Jesus as the focus? The answer is none! The tendency in ministry and in church life is to make some other good things the focus. We unite under our focus on missions, or reaching children and youth, or building a facility, or passing out Bibles, the kind of music we like, or some popular person or group in the church. And what happens? Eventually people disagree, start to fight over little things and lose sight of the mission they were on. They quit, leave, give up, or stay and do nothing but cause problems. Too often leaders blame it on individuals who could not grasp the vision. However, the real problem is that the leader or the group did not set their focus squarely on Christ Jesus.

When you and those you lead have their focus on Christ it becomes much more likely that you will be able to keep the unity you have in Christ. Beyond that, when the focus is on Jesus, all those other good things like outreach, missions, buildings, and great worship happen. This happens not because a church is united under a person, or a cause, but instead because they united under the Savior of the world. This is the leader's goal in unity. Make Jesus the focus of your life and the focus of your group and you will find that a spirit of unity will follow.

Later in Ephesians four, the writer goes into more specific detail about what the leader's role is in God's church and with God's people. While this passage is primarily directed at pastors and those who are called to be vocational ministers, it is important for all church leaders to understand this principle for two reasons. The first reason is so that you can better understand why those who lead the church lead the way they do. And secondly, so you can help them accomplish this amazing task! As a leader in your church God has gifted you and called you to help the staff in a direct supporting role. You too have a responsibility when it comes to keeping the unity in the church. This is what he says:

> Ephesians 4:11–16 (NET)—[11]*It was he who gave some as apostles, some as prophets, some as evangelists, and some as pastors and teachers,[12]to equip the saints for the work of ministry, that is, to build up the body of Christ,[13]until we all attain to the unity of the faith and of the knowledge of the Son of God— a mature person, attaining to the measure of Christ's full stature. [14]So we are no longer to be children, tossed back and forth by waves and carried about by every wind of teaching by the trickery of people who craftily carry out their deceitful schemes. [15]But practicing the truth in love, we will in all things grow up into Christ, who is the head. [16]From him the whole body grows, fitted and held together through every supporting ligament. As each one does its part, the body grows in love.*

According to this passage the leader's main role is to prepare God's people for works of service. This is so the body of Christ may be built up until we all reach unity in the faith.

As a leader in the church, God has called you to be a part of this amazing mission. Pastors and leaders are primarily equippers. They equip the saints so that the body may be built up. As a leader in God's church you equip and build others up so all the parts can come together and work as a unit for the glory of God. It is not your job to do all of the work, but instead to train and equip others to help in the work of the gospel. Workers work hard at doing the work and leaders do too, but leaders work even harder at building a team of others around them and training them to work in the ministry. You are not fully meeting your leadership potential until you become an equipper of others.

This passage focuses on another important aspect of unity. It states in verse thirteen that unity is a mark of maturity. New ministry teams and churches seem to have a lot of problems with unity. Why? Because they are generally full of immature believers. New churches are generally full of non-believers, recent converts, or people who have not actively been following Christ for years. As a result of their immaturity, unity is often hard to come by. They are full of indi-vidualism and selfishness, both of which never lead to unity. Unity can only be achieved to the degree that those you lead are mature in their faith. Unity is a mark of maturity in a believer's life and in the life of a team.

Think back to our young Spartan boys at the age of 7 as they were being taken from their parents home and thrown into a bar-racks with fifty other boys their own age. Do you think they were equipped to fight as a unit? Could they have defeated an attacking army? Of course not! They were immature, and fighting as a unit would have been impossible. Time, effort, and training led them to become a mature fighting force ready to fight as a unit. Maturity and unity walk hand in hand in the Kingdom of God. This is why the Apostle Paul linked them together in Ephesians.

With this in mind, you should make it your goal to not only keep the focus on Jesus at all times for your team, but to also help them mature in their faith. You do this by teaching them to keep their own focus on Jesus. This is why the statement was previ-ously made that the *first* thing you must do is make Jesus your focus. You cannot teach others to do what you have not been able to achieve yourself.

Jesus spoke of unity in His prayer recorded in John 17 which says:

> **John 17:20–23 (NET)**—[20]*"I am not praying only on their be-half, but also on behalf of those who believe in me through their testimony,* [21]*that they will all be one, just as you, Father, are in me and I am in you. I pray that they will be in us, so that the world will believe that you sent me.* [22]*The glory you gave to me I have given to them, that they may be one just as we are one—*[23]*I in them and you in me—that they may be completely one, so that the world will know that you sent me, and you have loved them just as you have loved me.*

His prayer is in part that Christians should all be one in complete unity. The words used here in the Greek text (*eis hen*) mean that we will be brought "into oneness" or that we would be one single liv-ing thing. This is the greatest mark of maturity that any church or group of believers can attain. This kind of oneness is rare and must be inspired and directed by God. The prayer that Jesus prayed could never be accomplished by a human leader alone, for he prayed that we would be one in the same way he and the father are one. In other words that we might be one in the same way the Holy Trinity[10] is one. This kind of holy unity means that we become so united that we are no longer just a group of individuals all doing the same thing, but instead we are the Body of Christ united in every way and functioning in harmony with all other parts of the body. This kind of unity brings honor and glory to God because it shows the world the love and compassion of Christ. It shows the world that it is not about us, instead it is about Him.

UNITY ASSASSINS

There are at least six unity assassins that I see at work in churches and teams all the time. As a leader you should constantly be on guard, and if you see one or more of these assassins approaching do whatever you can destroy it before it destroys whatever unity your team has.

The first assassin is "pride and arrogance." This can creep into the leaders life or the life of individual team members. Equally true is that entire teams can become prideful and arrogant which in the end leads to the destruction of unity. Scripture is clear: *Pride comes before destruction, and an arrogant spirit before a fall.*[11]

The next assassin is extremely dangerous and goes by the name "unforgiveness." All teams have struggles, disagreements, and difficulties. Feelings get hurt, heated debate takes place, and people say and do things that they normally would not. Whatever the cause, there will be a need for forgiveness to take place among members of your team. If this problem is ignored or dismissed it will kill the unity of your team.

---

10   The Holy trinity refers to Jesus Christ the Son, God the Father, and the Holy Spirit being unified together as one while each still having unique roles and characteristics.

11   Proverbs 16:18 (HCSB)

"Selfishness" is another assassin of unity. I was once naive to the horrible effects of selfishness. I thought that selfishness was when someone failed to consider and value others. After being in ministry for over two decades, I have concluded that selfishness is much worse. Selfishness is the act of a person or group of people not only thinking solely about themselves, but expecting everyone else to "only" think about them, too. Selfishness always leads to manipulation, power struggles, fights, quarrels, and the loss of unity.

Unbiblical conformity will destroy teams. Biblical conformity happens when everyone is trying to be like Jesus. Unbiblical conformity is the result of everyone being forced to be like anything else. When your team attempts to make everyone conform to the same mold and fit inside of the same template unity will be destroyed. God has made everyone different and equipped all the members of His family with unique gifts. We should celebrate our diversity while striving to be like Jesus, not minimize our differences while trying to be like something else.

Proverbs 16:28 says *"A perverse person spreads dissension, and a gossip separates the closest friends."* Gossip may be the worst and most active unity assassin of all. Gossip destroys teams, churches, friendships, families and anything else if given the opportunity. As a leader you must kill this unity assassin as quickly as possible or it will in short order destroy your team.

"Cowardness" is the final assassin. Edmund Burke is quoted as saying, "The only thing necessary for the triumph of evil is for good men to do nothing."[12] When leaders and other Christians refuse to stand up and confront the assassins who approach with evil intent teams and churches are destroyed. As a leader, you must confront evil, defend the faith, and never give a single inch of ground to the enemy. Proverbs 25:26 says, *"Like a muddied spring and a polluted well, so is a righteous person who gives way before the wicked."*

Unity assassins are extremely dangerous but only if they are not spotted early and stopped quickly. An assassin's main advantage is stealth and surprise. As a leader you must always scan the horizon and

---

12   http://www.brainyquote.com/quotes/quotes/e/edmundburk377528.
html#7rWDdTsqCjSdq6mc.99

never let your guard down. When you spot a unity assassin approaching your camp, take the threat seriously and respond accordingly.

KEYS TO KEEPING UNITY

So what can you do as a leader to help keep the unity in the church? First, handle conflict, disagreements, and other issues in the group as quickly as possible. It is tempting to just let something fester. We often say, "I want to take time to pray about it." This usually really means, "I don't want to deal with it and if I wait long enough maybe it will go away." While it may disappear for a while, it never really goes away. Sometime in the future this issue will arise again and involve more people, be more complex and much more difficult to deal with. Leaders don't seek out confrontation, but they must face it and deal with it head-on if the situation arises. Deal with issues, disagreements and conflict in honesty, with openness, and as quickly as possible to maintain the unity of the group.

Secondly, be careful to select good helpers and other leaders to surround you. These should not be people who say YES to everything you say, or give you their rubber stamp. They should be people you can trust, depend on, and turn to in times of need. They should be men and women who can hold you accountable as a leader too. If you have a strong team around you, turn to them quickly for advice and help when the unity of your group is threatened.

Next, do not accept or tolerate gossip on any level or from any person on the team. Make it clear from the example you lead in your own life that this harmful practice will not be accepted on your team. During team meetings, if someone talks about another team member or begins to gossip, you must kill it quickly or it will soon spread and cause the unity of the team to decay. If you hear gossip in the community about any staff member, church leader, or the church itself, you must stand up and put an end to it quickly. Gossip destroys unity and if you don't set the record straight, who will?

Strong teams also find it possible to 'agree to disagree' at times. No group of people will agree all of the time and few groups will agree most of the time. But with the right focus, teams can 'agree to disagree' on issues without affecting the unity of the group. Teach the importance of acceptance, and flexibility to those you lead. In Acts 2 it says, *"All the believers were together and had everything in common."* How could this be? There is no way they had everything in common, or did they? This young church no doubt had their disagreements, fights, and issues at times, but they also had the right focus. They were focused on Jesus Christ, and when He is the focus of each individual's life and the focus of the team, you will always have everything in common. Keep Jesus as the focus and you will find it not only possible to disagree and keep the unity, but indeed it will become natural.

CHAPTER SUMMARY

It is not the leader's job to create unity, instead every believer is called to maintain the unity that flows to believers naturally though the unifying blood of Christ. We must make every effort to make Christ the focus of our lives and the focus of our teams. Unity is more than a great idea or a wonderful concept. It is a powerful tool that can many times ensure victory before you even see the enemy. Satan attacks those who are weak and those who lack unity. A united team, or a united church, is very hard to defeat. Protect and maintain the unity of the church at all costs!

Final Questions

1. Is it your job as a leader to create unity? Why or why not?

2. What must a leader focus on to keep the unity?

3. What is unity a mark of? Why?

4. What are some practical things you can do to keep the unity of your group?

5. Have you seen the positive effects of unity in a team or church before? Explain.

6. Have you seen the negative effects that come with a lack of unity before? Explain.

7. Do you think the oneness Jesus prayed for is possible here on earth? If not why? If so explain how?

8. Have you ever had an encounter with one of these unity assassins? Which one and what was the result?

CHAPTER 11

——— Are You Ready?... ———

Serve wholeheartedly, as if you were serving the Lord, not men...—Ephesians 6:7

Are you ready to serve? Spiritual leadership is impossible if you are unwilling to serve others. Unfortunately, we live in a world that constantly tells us we should serve ourselves and look out for our own interests. Selfishness, however, always leads to the same place—division, and destruction. If you are unwilling to serve, you will not last long as a leader in God's Kingdom.

There is a story about a famous orchestra conductor named Leonard Bernstein who was once asked the following question. "Mr. Bernstein, what is the most difficult instrument to play in the orchestra?" Without hesitating for a moment, he replied with quick wit, "Second fiddle. I can get plenty of first violinists, but to find one who plays second violin with as much enthusiasm, or second French horn, or second flute, now that's a problem. And yet if no one plays second, we have no harmony."[13]

Great leaders are excited to be a part of the orchestra; they are not concerned with their position as much as they are with their part in making the music. Servant leaders enjoy the sound of the

---

13 Stephen A. Macchia, *Becoming a healthy disciple: ten traits of a vital Christian* (Grand Rapids, Mich.: Baker Books, 2004), 127.

orchestra more than they do the sound of their own horn. One of the most tragic verses in all of scripture is found in Luke's account of the Lord's Supper. It says in Luke 22:24, *Also a dispute arose among them as to which of them was considered to be greatest.* "Even within sight of the cross, we find the humanness of the disciples oozing out of their most intimate of community experiences."[14] How sad it is that on their last night together the disciples were still more concerned with the sound of their own horns, rather than the will of the conductor and sound of the orchestra.

We can see a great example of a servant leader in the life of Joseph in the fourth chapter of Acts. The name Barnabas was given to Joseph by the apostles because Barnabas means "Son of Encouragement" and that is the kind of man he was. Barnabas was the kind of man who was willing to build others up without giving any thought or consideration to his own needs or desires. He was more concerned with the effectiveness of the band rather than the individual instrument he played. We see this all through the book of Acts as we follow the life of Barnabas.

We learn in Acts four that the early church was in big trouble. They were under the stress of persecution. There were many in the church who had lost their jobs, or their ability to make money because they had converted to Christianity. So Barnabas sold some land and brought the money to the church to be used to meet the needs of others (Acts 4:32-37). He did not have to do this, no one made him sell his property and bring all of the money to the church. However, the working of the Spirit in his life compelled him to do this incredible thing and practice generosity in a way that few in the history of the world ever have. He put his own needs aside for the betterment of the church community. In doing this, he encouraged the church.

Barnabas was a respected leader in the early church. Saul on the other hand was a despised enemy of the church. Saul, who would later be known as Paul, was busy persecuting the church and even overseeing the death of some Christians (Acts 7:58). In the ninth chapter of Acts, Saul has an encounter with the resurrected Jesus

---

14   Ibid., 129

Christ on the road to Damascus and ultimately converts to Christianity himself. After spending three years in the desert (Galatians 1), Paul attempts to join the disciples in Jerusalem (Acts 9:26-28). The disciples, however, were afraid and unwilling to accept him fearing that he might just be trying to infiltrate the group to destroy the church. But Barnabas bridges the gap and through his influence brings Paul into the group. Barnabas risked all of his hard earned influence once again for the sake of the church taking a tremendous risk on Paul.

Barnabas and Paul would do a great deal of ministry together and through the encouragement of Barnabas, one of the greatest missionary and church planters the world has ever known, was trained. In the thirteenth chapter of Acts there is a major shift in the roles of Barnabas and Paul. It is here that Paul becomes the leader and Barnabas becomes Paul's co-leader. Barnabas does not complain or try to hold to his position, or control the group, instead he continues to encourage Paul. Barnabas is as content playing second fiddle as he was playing the lead part.

In Acts fifteen Barnabas has a strong desire to encourage John Mark. John had quit on a previous missionary journey (Acts 13:13) and Paul was unwilling to give him another opportunity to join the group. Barnabas, on the other hand, saw potential in John Mark and the disagreement between Paul and Barnabas caused them to disband and go in different directions. Barnabas and John went to Cyprus while Paul, Luke, and Silas set out for Syria, and Cilicia. Again, Barnabas was not concerned with getting his own way instead he sought a resolution that would allow both men to continue to work for God.

When Barnabas encouraged the church, he lost his land. When he encouraged Paul and brought him into the group of disciples, he lost his leadership position to Paul. And when he encouraged young John Mark, he lost his place in scripture and history. We never hear of Barnabas again after he departs for Cyprus, because Luke, who would write the book of Acts, went with Paul.

We do however hear about John Mark. He wrote the earliest Gospel in the New Testament, we know it as the book of Mark. Mark was a strong leader in the early church and through his ministry many were won to the faith. We also hear about Mark in the very last book that Paul wrote. Just before his death, in writing to Timothy, Paul writes *"Get Mark and bring him with you, because he is a great help to me in ministry."* (2 Timothy 4:11).

Mark was useful to Paul's ministry because of Barnabas. Paul was useful in the Kingdom of God because of Barnabas. Because Barnabas was willing to play second fiddle God was able to do amazing things. Barnabas was a servant, and without the selfless life of Barnabas it is doubtful that the church of God would be what it is today.

There are many other great leaders in the Bible and each of them can be described as a servant. Jesus is the best example of what servant leadership looks like. Paul wrote this about Jesus in the book of Philippians:

> **Philippians 2:1–11 (NET)**—*[1]Therefore, if there is any encouragement in Christ, any comfort provided by love, any fellowship in the Spirit, any affection or mercy, [2]complete my joy and be of the same mind, by having the same love, being united in spirit, and having one purpose. [3]Instead of being motivated by selfish ambition or vanity, each of you should, in humility, be moved to treat one another as more important than yourself. [4]Each of you should be concerned not only about your own interests, but about the interests of others as well. [5]You should have the same attitude toward one another that Christ Jesus had, [6]who though he existed in the form of God did not regard equality with God as something to be grasped, [7]but emptied himself by taking on the form of a slave, by looking like other men, and by sharing in human nature. [8]He humbled himself, by becoming obedient to the point of death—even death on a cross! [9]As a result God exalted him and gave him the name that is above every name, [10]so that at the name of Jesus every knee will bow—in heaven and on earth and under the earth— [11]and every tongue confess that Jesus Christ is Lord to the glory of God the Father.*

Jesus Christ took on the very nature of a servant, shouldn't we? After all, we are the disciples of Christ. The world is watching and listening to us. What do they see and hear? Are we servants or are we self-indulged, prideful individuals seeking position and power? No matter how hard you try, if you are the latter you will be exposed. The church needs individuals who are willing to serve others at all levels but it starts with the leadership.

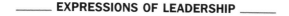

EXPRESSIONS OF LEADERSHIP

One of my seminary professors, Ebbie Smith, once outlined five specific things that express servant leadership as it relates to one volunteer leading another. These are the marks of a servant leader. See how many you can identify with.

The first is *relationship rather than position*. Servant leaders are relationship builders. They love and care about those they lead. Servant leaders don't use people simply as a means to achieve something. Instead, they value and are concerned about those they lead. Servant leaders understand that it is not their position that earns them the right to lead, but instead, it is relationships.

Service rather than control is the second expression of servant leadership. The natural temptations for those in leadership is to control and manage those we lead. They work for us, we are the leader for a reason, they should be willing to follow! But servant leaders do not seek control, rather they seek to serve those they lead. They find ways to provide, care, and love those they shepherd, and it's through service that they earn the right to lead.

The third expression of servant leadership is that the servant leader also focuses on *equipping rather than performing*. Leaders who insist on doing all the work themselves often say things like, "it's faster if I just do it" or "it's easier" or "I wanted it done right so I did it myself." In all honesty, one leader to another, they are right. It is faster, easier, and better if you do it yourself. But that kind of leadership is based on performance. Why are we so concerned with how fast or well something is done? So we can impress others around us and show them how well we perform as a leader? A true servant leader however is someone who equips and trains those they lead to help in the ministry.

Guidance rather than manipulation is the fourth expression of servant leadership. Too many leaders within the church try to lead by manipulating or tricking others. They will leave out certain information to sway the group one way or the other. They will neglect to tell both sides of a story. At times they flat out lie to "lead" the group in a direction they wish to go. Servant leaders, however, practice guidance rather than manipulation. They seek to guide those they lead in the right direction and trust that ultimately God is in control.

Finally, the servant leader is one who *pulls rather than pushes.* The servant leader does not try to push, poke, and herd people in a certain direction. Instead, they pull or lead the group by example. Here is an exercise you can do or just imagine in your mind. Take a single piece of string. Lay it on a flat surface and "push it." You will find that it is impossible to push without the string wadding up. Now take your finger and place it at one end of the string and begin to pull it. The string will go wherever your finger leads it. This is the difference between pushing and pulling those you lead. If you try to push them, you will have a mess on your hands. Get out front, set the example, and lead them as a servant and you will find that your team will follow you wherever you go.

SERVANT LEADERSHIP PRINCIPLES

At this point you might be saying, "Am I really ready?" I want you to understand that servant leadership is not something that comes naturally to any of us. It is something we learn through experience, wisdom, prayer, and being obedient to God. Entire books have been written on the subject of becoming a servant leader. And even if you read all of them you would still not feel ready for leadership. Being a leader is not something you can ever be fully ready for, instead it is something you are called to do. We can only accept or reject the call to lead that God places on our lives.

_____ PRINCIPLES OF SERVANT LEADERSHIP _____

For the purpose of our leadership training I would like to outline seven key principles that are important. These seven principles can be found in Gene Wilkes' book entitled *Jesus on Leadership*.[15] These principles will ensure that you are well on your way to becoming a servant leader should you choose to implement them into your life.

Principle one is *humble your heart*. Servant leaders are willing to humble themselves and allow God to praise them. In our world we often try to lavish praise and honor upon ourselves. The servant leader is not concerned with what others think or who is praising their efforts. Instead, they serve the KING of KINGS and LORD of LORDS and trust that He will exalt them.

Servant leaders must also learn to *first be a follower*. Our natural tendency is to equate positions and titles with leadership. This is typically how our world works; it is not, however, the way God works. Spiritual leaders are servants who must first learn the value of following other men and women and most importantly they must learn to follow God before they should expect to lead. There is no leader in God's kingdom who is not also a follower.

The third principle for servant leadership is to *find greatness in service*. Leadership will always require sacrifice. You will have to give up personal rights and pleasures in order to lead. Servant leaders find greatness in service rather than seeing it as a burden. Leaders who focus on the burden and sacrifice alone tend to burn out and fall away quickly. Servant leaders must learn to be content in any situation God places them in and find greatness in service to God alone.

Next Wilkes points out that leaders *take risks*. True servant leaders can risk it all because they trust God. Leadership is inherently risky. It has never been, nor will it ever be safe. Leaders are the first in and last out. Leaders are the biggest targets for the enemy. Leaders carry the heaviest load, and must deal with the most stress. The success or failure of a mission or project ultimately depends on the leader

---

15   C. Gene Wilkes, *Jesus on leadership* (Wheaton, Ill: Tyndale House, 1998), 25-27.

and their ability to manage and take risks. A servant leader learns to trust God and take risks.

Servant leaders must also *take up the towel*. Jesus washed the feet of those He led just before He was crucified. In doing so He set the example for servant leadership. Servant leaders are willing to bow down and do things that others are not. God's leaders are willing to do the hard and dirty work that is required. These kinds of leaders never ask those they lead to do anything they themselves would not do. Jesus was the last person in that room that should have picked up the towel that night. The irony is He was the first. He showed each of us what servant leadership looks like.

Servant leaders also *share responsibility and authority*. Servant leaders give the ministry away to those they lead. They equip, train, and build up those on their teams. Leaders must avoid keeping all of the responsibility and authority in their own hands at all times. This cripples the ministry and those they lead. Give away tasks, responsibility, and authority to those you lead once they are ready.

Wilkes points out that the seventh and final principle is *building a team*. Leaders are only leaders if others are following. Building a team is difficult and will test a leader's patience, but it is necessary. Servant leaders multiply and increase their leadership by building a team of people around them and equipping them to do the ministry. The true test of your leadership comes once you are gone. All of us will one day be gone for one reason or another. The servant leader who has built a team will see his or her ministry and legacy live on because they took the time to build a team and equip them to survive on their own.

CHAPTER SUMMARY

Servant leadership is not easy and will not come naturally. Leadership is something you must work on and develop as a part of your lifestyle. A true leader in the Kingdom of God must learn the value of servanthood before he or she will become a leader that leaves a legacy. Your success as a leader will not be based on your ability to lead. It will depend much more on your willingness to serve. Are you ready?

Final Questions

1. Explain why all leaders must first learn to follow.

2. What leadership issues are you facing at this time? Can any of the seven principles help those situations?

3. List some people in the Bible who were servant leaders and the principles of servant leadership you see in their lives.

4. Which principle will be the hardest for you and which will be the easiest? Why?

5. What do you think of when you hear the words "servant leader"?

6. List some of the ways Jesus served those he led. What can you learn from these examples? How do they apply to your team?

7. Which of the five expressions of leadership comes most natural for you?

8. Which of the five expressions of leadership are the most difficult for you?

CHAPTER 12

THE PASTOR'S PERSPECTIVE

Elders who provide effective leadership must be counted worthy of double honor, especially those who work hard in speaking and teaching. For the scripture says, "Do not muzzle an ox while it is treading out the grain," and, "The worker deserves his pay." Do not accept an accusation against an elder unless it can be confirmed by two or three witnesses.—1 Timothy 5:17–19 (NET)

It would be impossible to claim that I can speak for all ministers when it comes to what they would want their leaders to hear in this section. However, after serving as a full-time minister for so many years, and working alongside of hundreds of other pastors I feel an attempt should be made. This chapter is not about gaining sympathy for ministers, nor is it an attempt to glorify them. My genuine desire is to help you as a leader understand your minister, his job, why he needs your help, and how you can best help him. Furthermore, my prayer is that after reading this chapter, you will be less likely to unknowingly step on landmines that can harm your ministers.

As a leader in your church, you are an extremely important person to your pastor. He values your opinion, service, friendship, and support more than you will ever know. While you have more power than most to bless your pastor, you can also inflict the most pain, frustration, and genuine spiritual sorrow upon him. So, in this chapter, I hope to be honest, open, and informative so you can understand what your minister needs from you.

There is one last thing I would like to clearly state in this initial section. My family and I have been very fortunate to serve in a church that loves and respects their ministers. The members of Cowboy Fellowship have been true examples of what it means to bless their pastors. It is my prayer that I have been equally faithful in my attempts to serve them.

This chapter was not written in frustration, or as a response to something that happened in my personal journey as a minister. Rather I genuinely prayed that I might be able to sum up the larger perspective of ministers I have known and the struggles most ministers face.

_____ 21 THINGS YOU MIGHT NOT KNOW ABOUT _____ YOUR PASTOR & HIS FAMILY[16]

Able Baker is the lead pastor of Fort St. James Evangelical Free church and he has put together a list of twenty one things you might not know about your pastor and his family. As you read this list you should understand that most pastors do not experience all twenty-one of these things; however, all pastors experience many of them. Don't try to imagine which of these your pastor is struggling with. This list is presented so you have a better perspective of the issues pastors face.

1. He cannot afford the books he just bought to help him serve you better.

2. He has worked over five weeks in a row without a day off several times this year, and the only ones who know this are his wife and kids.

16 Baker, Able. "21 Things You Might Not Know About Your Pastor & Family." ChurchLeaderscom. August 06, 2014. Accessed February 25, 2015. http://www.churchleaders.com/pastors/pastor-articles/175638-able-baker-things-you-might-not-know-about-your-pastor-family.html.

3. Yes, he probably knows all the gossip about you, and loves you like family anyway.

4. He is always on call. If he has been a pastor for five years, he has been on call over 40,000 hours.

5. His children and wife hate the phone.

6. He has probably visited or received help from the food bank this year.

7. He can't sleep without some kind of medication.

8. He is probably on or has been on some kind of antidepressant.

9. He is probably not telling the truth about certain personal theological changes because he's afraid you will fire him.

10. He and his wife cannot afford childcare and a date at the same time. So they have probably not been alone together for months.

11. He is the loneliest person in the church, no matter how many friends he has. He can only allow certain people to become very close to him, and if he's smart, it's not a person in the congregation.

12. He wants to hide after every sermon.

13. His hardest day is Monday.

14. He has performed many weddings, funerals and counseling sessions for free. Most of the time it's the wealthy and middle-class families that don't pay or pay very little.

15. He wears the same clothes all the time for several years because he cannot afford new ones.

16. His most feared question is, "Hey, what are you doing tomorrow?"

17. He loves to hear about your trip to Hawaii unless his wife is around.

18. If he seems defensive often, he is probably being attacked a lot.

19. He is human and wrestles with how to reconcile his humanity with your expectations.

20. He knows that most marriage counseling will end in the couple leaving the church.

21. His kids have never heard dad say "maybe tomorrow" to you like he has said it to them hundreds of times.

These twenty one things are not true of all ministers. In fact, I can honestly say that there are at least seven things on this list that I have not personally experienced during my time in ministry. However, there is nothing on this list that I can honestly say have not affected at least ten ministers I know.

I would also like to share a set of statistics to help you gain a deeper perspective concerning your ministers. These statistics were taken from a website that focuses on pastoral care. They were compiled from studies conducted by The Fuller Institute, George Barna, and Pastoral Care Inc. Let's consider some statistics about pastors:

1.   90% of the pastors report working between 55 to 75 hours per week.

2.   80% believe pastoral ministry has negatively affected their families. Many pastor's children do not attend church now because of what the church has done to their parents.

3.   33% state that being in the ministry is an outright hazard to their family.

4.   90% feel they are inadequately trained to cope with the ministry demands.

5.   90% of pastors said the ministry was completely different than what they thought it would be like before they entered the ministry.

6.   70% of pastors constantly fight depression.

7.   70% say they have a lower self-image now than when they first started.

8.   70% do not have someone they consider a close friend.

9.   40% report serious conflict with a parishioner at least once a month.

10.   50% of pastors feel so discouraged that they would leave the ministry if they could, but have no other way of making a living.

11.   70% of pastors feel grossly underpaid.

12.   50% of the ministers starting out will not last 5 years in full time ministry.

13. Only 1 out of every 10 ministers will actually retire as a minister in some form.

14. 94% of clergy families feel the pressures of the pastor's ministry.

15. 80% of spouses feel the pastor is overworked.

16. 80% of spouses feel left out and underappreciated by church members.

17. 80% of pastors' spouses wish their spouse would choose a different profession.

18. The profession of "Pastor" is near the bottom of a survey of the most-respected professions, just above "car salesman".

19. Over 1,700 pastors left the ministry every month last year.

20. Over 1,300 pastors are terminated by the local church each month , many without cause.

21. Many denominations report an "empty pulpit crisis". They cannot find ministers willing to fill positions.

#1 reason pastors leave the ministry—Church people are not willing to go the same direction and *follow the lead* of the pastor. Pastors believe God wants them to go in one direction but the people are not willing to follow or change.[17]

Now, if you are a lay leader, you might be trying to figure out why anyone would want to be a pastor. If you are a pastor, you might be feeling a bit overwhelmed after being confronted with these two lists and seeing the things you have felt for so many years put into words. Don't be discouraged, there is no greater calling or privilege in the world than to be commissioned by God to lead in His church. This is true for both the professional and lay leader.

For all of the heartache, trouble, trials, and frustration, ministry is the most exciting and eternally significant job there is on this side of heaven. The rest of this chapter is focused on helping you understand how you can help your ministers. Knowing how to bless, encourage, and help your pastor is the greatest gift you can ever give him and the best thing you can ever do for your church.

---

17 "Statistics for Pastors." Pastoral Care, Inc. Accessed February 25, 2015. http://www.pastoralcareinc.com/statistics/.

_____ SO WHAT CAN YOU DO? _____

One of the best ways to help your church is to help your ministers. If you really desire to see your church grow, help your ministers grow. If you want to have a healthy church, ensure that your ministers are healthy. If you want to see your church change, help your pastor lead the change. Pastors need everyone's prayers and support, but as a leader in your church, they desperately need yours. So, here are some simple, obvious, but frequently overlooked things you need to know as a leader to help your pastor and church.

One of the biggest things you can do is give your minister the benefit of the doubt before you jump to any conclusion. Support, defend, and speak in favor of your pastor until you have some kind of certain proof that what you have heard, sensed, or suspected is true. Ministers are not perfect, and they should always be humble enough to admit this truth. But they are rarely guilty of whatever rumor or suspicion that is floating around. They are not trying to change things to hurt the church or cause members to leave. They are not intentionally producing weak sermons. When a pastor says he can't meet with someone, he is not being rude. Rather, he is being honest about his schedule. Always assume the best about your ministers until you are proven wrong.

Next, don't use sarcasm in regard to their children, spouse, health, or personal time. Your minister may smile when you say "I wish I could find a job where I only had to work thirty minutes a week." Or when someone says "You're leaving for vacation again… why do we give you two weeks off when you only work one day a week?" Similar comments that seem funny to you in regard to his family, weight, or any other personal matter are extremely hurtful to him.

Pastors already feel guilty about going on vacation because there is so much to do at the church. They struggle to spend quality time with their children due to the number of evenings they have to work. Instead of making a silly comment, speak a word of encouragement to your minister in regard to these matters. Let them know you will pray for them while they are away. No minister enjoys witty comments or sarcastic remarks about their personal life. So, speak truth instead.

As a leader, you should never go around the ministers of your church. Secret meetings, private phone calls, or e-mails that attempt to circumvent your ministers' authority in anyway should be avoided. Believe it or not, this happens all the time, and it is only harmful and hurtful to both the minister and church. Instead of going *around* your ministers, go *to* them and talk things out. If they won't listen, then take another brother or sister in Christ (maybe a deacon or elder), and speak with your minister. But again, go *to* him, not *around* him.

Never put yourself in a position where you are going against your pastor. I am not saying that you should always agree with your minister. I am not saying that ministers are perfect and never need to be corrected. These situations do happen, and should be addressed. However, it should not be you against them. As a leader, you and your minister are on the same team. So, work as a team to solve whatever problem, issue, or concern has arisen. Don't create opposition; instead seek a resolution in a friendly and biblical way.

The next thing you can do is be a leader and choose to lead. Your minister trusts, respects, and has confidence in your ability to lead. So, be a leader. As a leader, you should understand the structure, mission, and values of your church. Furthermore, you should understand what your parameters are as a leader. Work within the structure and boundaries that have been set and lead your team. Don't expect your pastor to lead the team through you. You are the leader of this team, so lead it.

Help your pastor preach the gospel and fulfill the mission of your church. As a team leader in your church, you should never set your team up in isolation from the rest of the church. Your team should enhance what the church is doing. As a leader, you should help lead those on your team to fulfill the mission of the church and the purpose of the gospel through whatever ministry you have been called to lead.

Be a leader that gets people involved in ministry. One of the most frustrating things for ministers is to see so many people sitting in front of them on Sunday and so few serving in any capacity. Be a leader that brings people in, builds them up, trains them and then sends them out. Don't expect your pastor to build your team and bring you volunteers. He is expecting your help in this department. Get as many people involved in ministry as possible.

Show your pastor that his time is valuable too. When most people set up a time to meet with ministers, they naturally ask to meet in the evenings after work. This is understandable since people have jobs and taking off work early is not always easy to do. As a result, ministers frequently are away from their families five or more nights a week. So, if you need to speak with your pastor and are able, try to meet with him during the day. This shows your pastor that you value his time and care about his family. If the issue is important enough to pull him away from his wife and children, it should be important enough to take off work an hour early as well.

Compensate your ministers in a way that honors their service. Few churches have an abundance of money. Equally true is that few pastors are greedy, materialistic people. If they are, they should not be your pastor anyway because they are unfit for leadership in God's church (1 Timothy 3:3). I am not going to attempt to tell you how much you should pay your pastor, but you should make sure that you pay them well.

The old adage was that pastors should make whatever the starting salary for a teacher in town would be. I disagree, not because I am a pastor but because pastors are not teachers. I love teachers. My grandmother and mother were both educators for their entire careers. When I left for college, I was pursuing a degree to become a teacher. I married a teacher. I believe that teachers are underpaid based on the tremendous value they bring to our society.

That being said, your pastor is not a teacher. The average teacher works approximately 1500-1600 hours a year. The average pastor works 3,380 hours per year. The first year teacher generally has a bachelor's degree; most pastors have a master's degree when they enter ministry. Teachers are rarely called upon in the middle of the night to go to the hospital, asked to come home from vacation early for a funeral, or told to clean the restrooms. I don't ever see teachers mowing the grass at school, or leading the school board meetings. Your minister is expected to do all of this and more. He is a janitor, teacher, maintenance man, coach, bus driver, and superintendent all rolled into one. Do the best you can to pay your ministers well. They see the budget and know what the church places a priority on. Make sure they are one of those priorities.

Next, don't make your ministers pay for their books, conferences, cell phones, or gas. Give them a budget and set limits that the church agrees on, but you should invest into the education of your pastor. Sending him to a conference is not a vacation. It is an investment into the life of your church. Buying him books is not an expense. It is an investment into the life of your church. If you expect your minister to answer the cell phone when you call, pay for his cell phone bill. I promise you, he is using that phone far more for church than he is for personal use. If you want him to make hospital visits, participate in the association's activities, and attend community functions on behalf of the church, give him a mileage allowance. Your minister sacrifices a great deal to serve your church. Be a champion for making his job easier and making him better by doing the things mentioned above.

Here is another simple but important thing. Talk to your pastor about things that have nothing to do with church. He talks about church all day everyday. Your pastor is, after all, a normal person like you. He may not have much of a life outside of church, but there is something he would love to talk to you about. Find out what it is, and make it a point to invest in your pastors personal interests.

Thank your pastor publicly. Why not take a moment to post something positive about your pastor on social media? If you are given an opportunity to speak at church, say a kind word about the pastor. If you happen to be given a chance to speak in your community, say something positive about your pastor. When you speak well of your pastor publicly, it not only encourages him, it makes your church look great as well. It communicates we love each other to your community. There is a difference between pastor worship and thanking your pastor publicly, no pastor wants to be worshiped, but all deserve a little praise every now and then.

Don't expect your pastors full attention on Sunday morning before or after the church service. As a leader, you should have access to your minister anytime during the week. Don't wait until five minutes before church starts to engage him with some question about your ministry or ask him to make a last minute announcement for your team. He cares deeply about you and your ministry, but there is so much on his heart and mind both before and after church. Do your best to allow him to focus on the task at hand, send him an e-mail on Monday if you need to talk.

If you want to support your pastor and encourage him, then show up on Sunday morning. If you decide that going fishing, hunting, or shopping is more important than church that weekend, don't tell him about it or post it on social media where he will see it. Being in church on Sunday should be a priority for all church leaders. Your presence encourages your pastor and communicates that you value what the church is doing. Your absence does the opposite.

Take a punch or a bullet for your pastor. When you see a fight coming, get between your pastor and the attacker, and take the punch. Don't just have your pastor's back, get in front of him and defend him. If someone starts taking shots at your ministers in a business meeting, and the entire leadership team rises up, walks to the front, stands in unison, and says "we love our pastor, if you have an issue, you can address it with us as the leadership team of this church," your pastor and the church will never forget that moment. If you let your poor pastor stand there alone, humbly and helplessly enduring the barrage, your pastor and your church will never forget that moment either. Take a punch or bullet for your ministers so they can live to fight another day.

Don't bring your minister a problem that you have not already prayed about and tried to find a solution for. There are times when leaders need help solving problems. However, many times lay leaders don't attempt to solve a problem because they think their minister will have all of the answers. If you go to your pastor with a problem, you should already have some idea about what the solution is or made an attempt to fix the problem and failed. Your pastor can't solve every problem. You are a leader, and part of your responsibility is solving problems that come up in church.

Finally, if you want to help your pastor, read your Bible, pray, and grow as a disciple of Jesus Christ. Be the kind of leader who is always learning and striving to be better. Be positive and realistic in your pursuit of holiness, and let the light and life of Jesus pour out of you everyday. In doing this, you will bless, encourage, and help your pastor more than you will ever know.

———— **THINGS YOU SHOULD NOT EXPECT FROM YOUR PASTOR** ————

1. Don't expect him to be perfect.
2. Don't expect him to know everything about anything.
3. Don't expect him to do your job.
4. Don't expect him to be at your service 24 hours a day.
5. Don't expect him to always agree with you.
6. Don't expect him to forsake his ministry to his family to minister to yours.
7. Don't expect him to hit a grand slam every Sunday in the pulpit.
8. Don't expect him to keep everything the same.
9. Don't expect him to preach every Sunday.
10. Don't expect him to be like your last pastor.
11. Don't expect him to be successful without your help.
12. Don't expect him to survive as a minister without your help.
13. Don't expect him to thrive as a husband without your support.
14. Don't expect him to be a perfect father.
15. Don't expect him to be like that great pastor on TV, or like the one whose book you read last week.
16. Don't expect him to be involved in every school, social, and community event in your county.
17. Don't expect him to know what you are thinking.
18. Don't expect him to never fail.
19. Don't expect him to stop believing in you.
20. Don't expect him to stop pursuing God.

CHAPTER SUMMARY

Ministers protect, provide, guide, lead, and encourage those God places under their care. You are one of those people. However, as a leader in the church, you are also expected to protect, provide, guide, lead, and encourage your minister. I can honestly say that as a minister, I have been more fortunate than most to serve a congregation of people who strive to do this. In their efforts to provide, protect, guide, and encourage me, I am constantly inspired to reciprocate those actions myself. In so doing, our relationship as minister and lay leader is strengthened, and the church is enhanced as well.

If you look at the truly great churches that are able to accomplish wonderful things by the grace of God, you will find that they all have this one thing in common. They all have a great team of leaders like you. Sure they have great ministers too, and that is who people normally see. But there is always a strong, vibrant, biblically sound team of spiritual lay leaders in these churches. These are people just like you who are protecting, providing, and helping those ministers on a daily basis.

God's church was never designed to be one where a single person could possess all of the gifts and talents necessary to produce success. From the very beginning, church was designed to function best, not around a person, but a team. You are on that team with your pastor. So, embrace the call as a leader, and embark on this journey with the minister God has placed in your church.

Questions To Consider

1. Why is it important for church leaders and ministers to have a strong relationship?

2. What are some things you can do this week to encourage your ministers?

3. What, on the list of "21 Things You Probably Don't Know About Your Pastor and His Family", surprised you?

4. Near the end of the chapter, there was a list of "20 Things You Should Not Expect From Your Pastor." What on this list have

you previously expected of your ministers? What have you seen others expect from pastors?

5. Why do you think it is important for leaders to take punches and bullets for their ministers? What kind of effect does this have on the church as a whole?

6. If you have a problem with your pastor what is the biblical way to handle it?

7. Why do you think it is important to give your ministers the benefit of doubt before jumping to conclusions?

Pete Pawelek is a pastor, author, church planter, and speaker. He earned a Bachelor of Arts in Communication with a minor in Religion from Texas State University. He obtained his Masters Degree (M.Div) from B.H. Carroll Theological. Pete is currently working toward earning his Doctorate from Logsdon Theological Seminary. Pete has worked extensively with youth, collegiate ministries, and mission organizations around the world. He is the author of *The Absolute Basics of Christianity*, *The Living Lamp*, and *The Uncommon Church*. Pete is currently the senior pastor of Cowboy Fellowship in Pleasanton, Texas where he lives with his wife Abby and their three children. You can contact Pete through his website, **www.pastorpete.org**.

Made in United States
Orlando, FL
31 May 2022

18363791R00074